Attitudes
and
Altitudes

The Dynamics of 21st Century Leadership

Pat Mesiti

EMBASSY BOOKS
www.embassybooks.in

Attitudes and Altitudes
The Dynamics of 21st Century Leadership

This edition licensed by arrangement with:
DreamHouse Publishing Pty. Ltd.
P.O.Box 50374, Waterfront 8002, South Africa.
Tel.: +27 21 4197704. Fax: +27 21 4198269

Published in India by :
EMBASSY BOOK DISTRIBUTORS,
120, Great Western Building,
Maharashtra Chamber of Commerce Lane,
Fort, Mumbai - 400 023.
Tel. : (91-22) 22819546 / 32967415
E-mail : info@embassybooks.in
Website: www.embassybooks.in

Printed & Bound in India by Quarterfold Printabilities, Navi Mumbai

ISBN 13: 978-81-88452-15-6

CONTENTS

Dedication

To the three women in my life: My wife Liz, and my two gorgeous daughters Rebecca and Chantelle

Thanks

I would like to thank Graeme Kirkwood, Bronwyn Hitzke, Craig Heilmann and Owen Salter without whose assistance this book would not have been possible.

INTRODUCTION

There is always a diverse response when you ask someone to define leadership. Many people say it is vision, courage, credibility or determination. But I sincerely believe leadership is first and foremost about people. It's about leaders releasing people to do what they need to do in the most productive and beneficial way. Leadership is about people from beginning to end.

You cannot call yourself a leader and not have followers. A leader's greatest compliment and achievement is his or her followers, and followers will reflect a leader's positive values and vision. The opposite is also true. Flawed leadership – for example, the lack of integrity that, sadly, we so often associate with today's leaders – will also reproduce itself in followers.

Our attitudes in leadership will determine the altitude of both our leadership and our followers. Attitude stirs passion and drive and results in empowerment. The practice of leadership principles reproduces great people. The power of leadership influences people.

Leadership is about people from beginning to end

More than anything else, leadership is about taking people somewhere. It's about giving direction, purpose, guidance and a sense of achievement. Therefore, the leader is a servant. Leaders help people achieve maximum impact in all their endeavours. If your goal is to motivate others to do greater things than you have done, then leadership is for you. Walter Lippman once said, 'The final test of a leader is that he leaves behind in other men the conviction and will to carry on.'

Leaders should treat others as though they were already where they should be. Leaders have to know where people should be going. Leaders help others to become what they are capable of being. Therefore, leaders must develop in themselves the skills which are essential to helping people achieve their goals. Leadership is always about relationship.

I communicate with many people through seminars and conferences, and I always make it my ambition to create a relationship with my audience; I endeavour to develop a connection with them. Otherwise, I can't really lead them anywhere. The same is true in building personal relationships with my staff: I try to help them maximise their human potential, to lead them into growth. Providing direction and relationship are two vital elements; both require specific skills.

This book is about building big people through relationships. The relational leader is one of the greatest needs of the hour. The leader who is able to relate, to unite, to encourage, to serve, is the leader who will launch other people to fulfil their potential in life. Relational leaders not only encourage people to do their best, but at times call upon them to reach beyond it and go further than their natural abilities. The relational leader will produce people who have the courage to tackle a task even if they do not possess expertise; they will do it anyway because the leader is able to rally them to the cause.

Leadership is about taking action and motivating others to do the same. Leadership is not just about holding a position or spouting what you believe. Positions and titles come and go. Action and relationship are the marks of true leadership, and they last forever.

Without people there can never be leadership. People are the heart, soul and spirit of any organisation. Without them there is no need for leaders. Leaders are therefore responsible to see people use their assets. They are the ones responsible for the next generation of leadership. They need to focus on what people can be. They must identify future potential, harness it, develop it, train it up, feed it ideas, information and vision, and motivate it. Without such motivation people will go nowhere.

The relational leader must realise that people are continually evolving. I believe in the development and evolution of every human being's leadership abilities. People are always in a constant state of change and development. They are either increasing or diminishing in their effectiveness. Good leaders relate well to followers and will train and equip them, growing them into valuable and industrious people.

> *'The function of leadership is to produce more leaders, not more followers'*
> **Ralph Nader**

Leaders must keep people fuelled and fed to enable them to maximise their capabilities as well as overcome their deficiencies. To do this, leaders must understand they have to build relationships. In achieving anything great, relationships are far more important than either structure or management. Structures have almost nothing to do with establishing trust and respect.

People begin to maximise their potential when they come into bonded relationship with leaders who are willing to take the time to develop trust. Trust stems from relationship and is the product of people-to-people skills, not structure or hierarchy. Trust is the organisational glue which bonds people together. You can be the boss and the structure will support you, but growing big people is about trust. Warren

Bennis and Bert Nanus have wisely written, 'Trust is the emotional glue that binds followers and leaders together.'

It is amazing to see a football team which, though replete with champion players, loses to a championship team. One is a team of champions; the other is a champion team. The relational leader will not just build a team of champions but a championship team. Such a team will flow and work together on the basis of mutual trust and respect.

No team grows on individual vision and drive, but on corporate vision and drive. This is a true recipe for success. Corporate vision builds interdependence rather than independence. Leaders who help people to become interdependent, to work together as well as to be successful individually, build strong teams. Such a leader realises that no individual has all the answers, nor all the gifts or talents.

In this book you will discover how to bring out the best in people, both as individuals and as a team. You will discover the dynamic principles for successful leadership. Through mastering these

'The growth and development of people is the highest calling of leadership'
Harvey S. Firestone

you will begin to build big people and your vision will grow one-hundred-fold.

This is a book of principles to live by. I often say, 'Life is a series of principles - if you practise the principles, you will profit from the principles you practise.' Try saying that after a peanut butter sandwich!

But listen: the relational leader is a builder of big people and big dreams. He or she is able, in the immortal words of *Star Trek*, to motivate people 'to boldly go where no one has gone before.' John D. Rockefeller had it right when he said, 'Good leadership consists in showing average people how to do the work of superior people.'

'No one of us is as smart as all of us'
Ken Blanchard

The 21st century leader, the relational leader or whatever you may wish to call him or her, is not just interested in people reaching goals. He or she wants them to reach their potential and destiny. Anything less is just not good enough.

That's why leadership is also about service. There are times when you need to give strong direction to people who have lost their way or purpose. Sometimes you need to encourage and support. At other times leadership means to consult and advise. Leaders draw out the latent abilities within other people. Leadership happens even when followers cannot see these abilities in themselves. But leaders always desire to serve.

All in all, the leader's role is extremely diverse, but it always requires these two ingredients: service and relationship.

Leaders also know when and how to take risks. Peter F. Drucker says, 'Courage, rather than analysis, dictates a truly important rule for identifying priorities. Pick the future against the past. Focus on opportunity rather than on problems, choose your own direction rather than climb on the band wagon and aim high, aim for something that will make a difference, rather than for something that is safe and easy to do.'

Have you ever noticed that when people speak of the negatives in leaders, they rarely list mistakes they have made? They relate more to such things as bad behavioural patterns. For instance, 'He's too busy to listen or advise me'; 'She takes all the credit'; 'He motivates by fear'; 'She always puts me down'; 'He's double-minded'. Such examples reflect poor relationship and poor behaviour. But people almost never criticise when a leader steps out, takes a risk and fails. So this book is also about courage, learning to step out and really lead from the front. Frederick Willcox has said, 'Progress always involves risk, you can't steal second base and keep your foot on first.'

Of course, saying that people don't remember your failings doesn't mean leaders should ignore them. We have a responsibility to our followers to be the best we can be. What's that you say? You're too busy to change? *You will have to find the time.* Leadership, remember, is about serv-

'I not only use all the brains I have but all that I can borrow'

Woodrow Wilson

ing. If you have been guilty of negative behavioural patterns, you can unlearn them. What's more, you can replace them with positive behavioural patterns. This book will help you do that, too.

Through practising these principles and learning them, I believe you will communicate better, motivate better, inspire better, and, above all else, relate better to people. You can become the leaders' leader. But don't try to be the boss; leadership has very little to do with that. The leader who tries to sit on a throne and lead with the philosophy of 'I am leader - you are plebs', needs to hear the words of Napoleon: 'The throne is only a bench covered with velvet.' So, be willing to learn a servant's heart as you read this book.

You can become the leaders' leader

And while we're on the subject of Napoleon, don't let me hear you say you're too busy to buy this book and read it:

Conquering the world with one hand, reforming it with the other, Napoleon used to dash from city to battlefield and back again in a manic fury of energy. His specially equipped carriage jounced down rutted roads while the diminutive Corsican sat inside, desperately scribbling - a whole new legal code before lunch, afterwards dozens of commands to his field marshals, proclamations, edicts, love letters.

Couriers raced to catch the hurtling carriage, bringing dispatches, then rushing off to deliver imperial epistles to the battlefield or to his archaeologists in

Egypt or to the Empress Josephine, comfy at home at Malmaison. When he had finished reading a document, Napoleon tore it to bits and tossed it out the window. Books too, once he'd looked at them, he hurled from the imperial conveyance like randomly lobbed artillery shells, so that the road, after the dust had cleared, was littered as if some demented Hansel had decided that this time there'd be no mistaking the path. (Time *magazine*)

If Napoleon had time to do all that and still keep in touch with his people, so can you.

Finally, why did I write this book? Because I have been a leader for many years and I am passionate about it. I have seen first-hand how a leader can influence others for the better. I have learned to be a relational leader, so this is not a book of theory. It's a book of doing, written for doers. Enjoy.

CHAPTER ONE

THE LEADER AND FOLLOWERS

The care of those you lead must always take priority over your own well-being. As a leader your primary goal is to accomplish your mission, but the welfare of your followers is your second priority. After all, without followers you're not a leader.

A leader induces followers to become leaders themselves and to perform more productively. A leader should help people to develop a greater sense of achievement and establish a sense of ownership. Achieving this requires positive people skills, such as understanding what motivates people and what enables them to accomplish given tasks, and knowing how to keep them loyal.

The leader must first understand, as Napoleon Hill did, that no successful individual becomes a success by himself or herself, or by any accomplishment that one can make alone. Hill discovered through his research that everyone who becomes a success does so with the help of others.

Ken Blanchard says, 'No one of us is as smart as all of us.' Everyone who has ever made it to the top has, at some time, benefited from the contribution of someone else into their life. Woodrow Wilson put it this way: 'I not only use all my brains but all that I can borrow.' Without that support, greatness and success become illusory.

I've know this in my own experience. I love to write books. However, typing is not one of my great strengths. Fortunately, my personal assistant, Bronwyn, says it's becoming one of hers. To get to where I'm going I need the assistance of Bronwyn and of my Business Administrator, Graeme – two people skilled in areas different to me.

This is the principle of *synergy* in operation: the sum total of our gifts and talents, working together, is greater than each and every individual part. Synergy is imperative in leadership, and good leaders know how to foster it.

Good leadership attracts others. Once leaders have attracted people, however, they must continually develop their skills, both to keep followers following and to launch them further. This means one of the greatest attributes a leader must have is *influence*.

Leaders help people work together for mutual benefit. Followers help leaders to reach goals, and, in doing so, leaders empower followers to reach their own goals. There is an exciting mutual dynamic at work.

No successful individual becomes a success by himself or herself

How do you get people to follow you? And how do you develop them so they keep following and eventually become leaders themselves? Here in this first chapter I want to outline some vital principles of relational leadership, based on three key concepts: *direction, significance and its effect* and *growing big people*.

ESTABLISH DIRECTION

One of the most important principles in achieving long-term, successful leadership is *establishing direction*. If you know and understand where you are going, people will follow you. It is sensible, therefore, to establish clear, concise direction.

Make sure your direction is measurable, consistent and achievable. Leadership is about taking people toward, and eventually arriving at, a destination predetermined by you. It is not about setting people up for failure.

Leaders who change direction constantly confuse their followers. Directionless leadership is no leadership at all. People cannot follow leaders who don't know where they are going.

But leaders who know where they are going enlist and keep quality people. Leaders must keep ahead of those following – but keep in view, too. Followers need to sense a strong, consistent direction.

Providing Direction

I recall recently driving behind a friend in another vehicle. He knows every short cut in the city, but he has a lead foot, and in peak hour traffic he is very hard to follow – especially when you don't know which way he's going to turn. Thank the dear Lord for cellular phones!

The point of this analogy is to reiterate again: you must let people know where you are taking them. Thomas A. Stewart said this in *Fortune* magazine: 'A prime reason leaders fail is that they rise to power with no understanding or training in how to use it.' You are in charge to provide direction – make sure you do.

In my own experience as leader of a large organisation, I build strong leadership by setting clear direction. As a result, our organisation has risen to new levels of success, achievement, innovation and creativity. My leadership team is composed of good people who understand our direction.

Setting direction is not about talking but about genuine training. Soldiers are not talked into fighting readiness; they are trained. They have hands-on experience and learn by doing.

Know, Grow and Show a Leader

John Maxwell has written a wonderful book, *Developing the Leaders Around You.* He writes, 'It takes a leader to know a leader, grow a leader, and show a leader.'

In the early school years, children do a little item called 'Show and Tell'. Leaders need to learn the kindergarten principle of 'show and tell'. Let me illustrate.

When I was younger, I worked at a factory with my Dad, he was in charge of the assembly line for a lawnmower company. I remember clearly the first day I looked at that assembly line. It seemed the worst task imaginable. I was placed beside someone who knew how to assemble a particular part of the lawn-mower. I had no experience at assembling anything, but he showed me how to do it. I watched him do it. He let me do it with supervision. He corrected my style – or lack of it! Then one day, I could do it. Next I taught someone else how to do it. Show and tell!

Leadership is about taking people toward, and eventually arriving at, a destination predetermined by you

As a leader established in relationship with followers, you must set direction for them. In doing so, you multiply yourself; and in multiplying yourself, you become all the more effective. In turn, those you train will produce other leaders who will be even more effective.

The foundation of all this is determining your own direction.

There are many organisations with great structure but poor leadership. They are guaranteed to fail. There are great organisations with inadequate structure – perhaps even poor structure – but they become great by having great leaders. Good leadership produces growth even in spite of structure. Why? Because leadership sets direction by developing relationships with followers. In turn, followers follow and bring goals to fulfilment.

Let me say it one last time for emphasis: To develop people and enlist them you must set the direction.

ESTABLISH SIGNIFICANCE

The second principle to understand is that followers require a *sense of significance*. Nothing motivates people more than the feeling that they are worthwhile and important.

This does not mean a leader manipulates through some hidden agenda. Leaders must genuinely believe followers *are* valuable and important.

When leaders are effectively communicating this, people rise up and take hold of their own challenges as well as

'A prime reason leaders fail is that they rise to power with no understanding or training in how to use it.'

Fortune magazine

those of the organisation. This sense of significance causes growth. Olympic hopefuls sense the call of significance, the clarion call to create their own moment of history, and they rise to the challenge and achieve their gold.

Making a Significant Contribution

Creating a feeling of importance and significance is a more powerful motivation than money, promotion or working conditions. When the money stops, people still want to make a significant contribution.

There was a time during our work with youth when we faced enormous financial pressure. However, not one of our team resigned, despite the difficult circumstances. They knew the heat was on, so what did they do? They turned up the heat and began to work even harder. They came up with creative ideas to expand and increase our effectiveness.

Why did they react like that? I believe it was because they felt they were making a difference in the lives of other people, regardless of the pay cheque.

Good leadership produces growth even in spite of structure.

As a leader it is up to you to engender this sense of significance – to give people a reason to keep on doing what they do. After all, the motivation for following is just as important as the direction you're going. In fact, it is probably more important, because the *reason* generates the *purpose*. That is why organisations which honour and acknowledge achievement will always have followers. They are giving people a sense of purpose and significance.

Why's and What's

Purpose and significance are the *why's* of an organisation. The *why's* and *what's* of an organisation must never be confused. Let me explain what I mean.

The why of an organisation is its *purpose* and *mission* – why you do what you do. This is what *motivates*. The *what* of an organisation is the specific tasks which must be done to fulfil the *why*. Purpose motivates; tasks accomplish. Always remember, tasks are never as motivating or as fulfilling as purpose. They are the grease on the cogs, but the cogs are the purpose. *What* needs to be done will be ignited by *why* we do it.

On many occasions I speak to dynamic meetings of Networkers. I have watched as people receive recognition and gain a sense of accomplishment through walking across the stage and receiving well-earned acknowledgment for their successes. This creates in them a feeling of significance and appreciation for their efforts. It motivates and encourages them to keep pursuing their short, medium and long-term goals. As they gain greater recognition, they gain a greater sense of success. Why? Because they understand they are important and respond accordingly.

The focus must always be a purpose. When follower and leader work together for a common purpose, a team spirit comes into operation. Followers in a team-relationship with leaders are not afraid to work hard to achieve their maximum potential if they are motivated by the call of significance.

Living for a Cause

One of our recent events attracted thousands of young people. As always, we offered counselling for those in need. I stood with one of my team members and we watched young people pour out their hurts, fears and struggles to the counsellors. One of my team said, 'I'd die for this.' I turned around and said, 'Go one better and live for it.'

That's the call of significance. It helps people to be creative and be alert to ideas on how to expand and complement their strengths and minimise their weaknesses.

WHAT SIGNIFICANCE DOES

Significance Creates Loyalty

The leader who imparts a sense of significance to his or her followers develops in them both individual and corporate loyalty. Their loyalty is marked by a willingness

Purpose motivates; tasks accomplish.

and a desire for personal change, even when it means pain or sacrifice.

They become 'stayers' not quitters, actively committed to the success and development of the organisation. Those with a 'hired hand' mentality come and go – they're in it for the job, the promotion. There's nothing wrong with that. But there's a greater quality the leader must both impart to, and extract from his followers – that of *faithfulness*.

As a leader, you cannot overestimate the value of creating a sense of significance in your followers. Loyalty will follow and in turn produce corporate significance, teamwork and unity. It also becomes a springboard to further success.

Subordinates or Supporters?

When signing The *Declaration of Independence,* Benjamin Franklin said, 'We must all hang together or else we shall hang separately.' Your team is not your *subordinate*; it is your *supporter*.

Niccolo Machiavelli once said, 'The first method for estimating the intelligence of a ruler is to look at the men he has around him.' When you give people a sense of significance, it not only lifts their spirits, it also resists against any sense of hierarchy.

If someone in an organisation or business feels they are a subordinate and consequently less. than others, they will function at a lower level of worth. I encourage you to ensure those following you don't feel like *subordinates* but *supporters*.

You must encourage them to be supporters of the vision, supporters of leadership. Likewise, you must be a supporter of *their* dreams, aspirations and goals.

As a result, you will develop an organisation with a common purpose. That purpose is not only the success of the organisation, but also the success of the individuals *within* that organisation, in all areas of life.

Significance Builds Teamwork

Growing a unified sense of purpose leaves no room for bitter rivalry among the team. Many of us have listened to the beautiful music of the Three Tenors. In an article published in *Atlantic Monthly* (Nov. 1994) a journalist kept pressing the issue of competitiveness among Carreras, Domingo and Pavarotti. Here's what Domingo said: 'You can't be rivals when you're together making music; you have to put all your concentration into opening your heart to the music.'

A faithful disposition in a leader, when imparted into a team, causes everyone to stay through thick and thin

The team must always be more important than my individual gratification. Henry Kissinger put it this way: 'What's causing so much disharmony among nations is the fact that some want to beat the big drum, few are willing to face the music, and none will play second fiddle.'

Leaders Inspire Teams to . . .

- *Vision* – see as a team
- *Unity* – stick like glue as a team
- *Friendships* – live as a team

- *Purpose* – aim as a team
- *Celebration* – win as a team
- *Openness* – communicate as a team
- *Empathy* – feel as a team
- *Productivity* – be effective as a team
- *Encouragement* – act as a team

Significance Produces Strength

People with a sense of significance do not operate from a position of weakness but from one of strength. Their hearts are set on supporting and strengthening their leader. They are united in their commitment to a singular purpose. They give their best, not because the leader motivates them, but because they are inwardly motivated.

When people have a sense of significance, they add value to the leader by placing value in themselves. In this way, organisations become strong and healthy, and followers grow into empowerment and fulfilment.

Significance Engenders Trust

Warren Bennis and Bert Nanus comment, 'Trust is the emotional glue that binds followers and leaders together.' When leaders impart a sense of significance, followers feel trusted. When they feel trusted they become trustworthy. So, when a follower's

'We must all hang together or else we shall hang separately'
Benjamin Franklin

ego gets in the way, he or she is able to put that aside, knowing that they are part of a purpose far bigger than personal ego.

'You can't be rivals when you're together making music; you have to put all your concentration into opening your heart to the music'

Domingo

It is amazing how leaders who inspire people to a purpose often reap purpose from them in return. Followers become encouragers. Often, when I have made an effort to inspire and encourage other leaders, to tell them how great they are and what an incredible job they are doing, they in turn seem to have just the right word to encourage me.

It is the very old principle of sowing and reaping. If you sow purpose and significance in people, you will reap a sense of purpose and significance. You are forming a bridge of relationship and trust which others will cross.

Ten principles for developing trust

1. *Allow for diversity within unity.*
2. *Give responsibility and praise results.*
3. *Express trust verbally and always be honest.*
4. *Praise publicly, reprimand privately.*
5. *Let them go, let them grow, let them learn.*
6. *Allow expression of ideas and creative implementation.*

7. *Encourage initiative.*
8. *Set boundaries of responsibility, delegation and authority.*
9. *Never reprimand when a line has not been clearly drawn.*
10. *Share the glory – don't hoard it.*

Significance Stimulates Accountability

Someone who has a sense of significance assesses their own performance and often knows when they are slipping in their level of commitment, efficiency and effectiveness. When someone has a sense of purpose, he or she will also monitor their own performance.

A sense of importance and significance creates in followers the desire to become better in *all* areas of work – to grow and expand in skill, knowledge, passion, vision and zeal. None of this comes without emotional struggle, but when they are pursuing a purpose with a sense of significance developed by their leader, they will not shy away from discomfort. Even if they do, the leader can help them face that challenge with a greater sense of purpose.

Overcoming Fears

At one of our Easter events we were grooming a new music team. One of the singers who was previously a backing vocalist found herself as the new leader of the vocal team.

This gifted and talented young lady felt a sense of fear at being up the front. Yet today, she is one of the most dynamic, 'on the edge' and radical leaders we've ever had at our events. What changed her from a background person to an up front person? A sense of purpose, responsibility and accountability. She broke through the emotional struggle, the discomfort of leadership, and now leading comes naturally.

Growing into Greatness

When leaders have a sense of purpose, they will know when and how to sharpen an axe. You can become totally exhausted cutting trees with a blunt instrument!

Sharpening axes is about ensuring that followers' values are incorporated into corporate values. A leader needs to know the desires and dreams of the people. I have often heard it quoted, 'People don't care how much their leader knows, until they know how much their leader cares' – how much he or she cares about *their* goals, dreams and desires.

Trust is the emotional glue that binds followers and leaders together

This is the catalyst for all success. It is important for leaders to find out what people want. As a leader in relationship with your followers, you must not only know what people need, but also what they must do to get to where they want to grow. Yes, that's right – I said 'to get to where they want to *grow.*' Not just 'go.' They need to *grow* into their dreams.

To achieve this, leaders must provide certain things

to help them grow. It's just like watering a plant. Leaders are gardeners. They must first give a sense of security. They do this by providing firm direction. Then they must give a sense of significance. They do this by imparting purpose. But they must also offer followers a mentoring relationship, and expose them to *helps* – books, tapes and speakers who will motivate them. Leaders must train, not just teach, followers in all areas of personal growth.

Believing in People

To give people a sense of accountability, leaders must believe in people as well as in their abilities. We must differentiate between the two. At times it is possible to believe in people but not their abilities. At other times, it is possible to believe in abilities but not the person.

To believe in people and their abilities requires intimacy and trust. Intimacy means getting close enough to know them.

Leaders must trust that people are capable of doing what is required of them. Leaders are patient. If someone is not capable at the moment, leaders offer the time and necessary input to assist them. Your time with followers grants them a sense of significance and trust, both of themselves and their abilities. It requires you to give of yourself as an investment in them.

Building Trust with Accountability

There are four keys to building trust with accountability:

1. *Open communication.*

2. *Sharing weaknesses and strengths.*
3. *Creating accountability through relationship, not rules.*
4. *Being open and vulnerable.*

The last key, vulnerability, may sound very weak, but let me describe what I mean. I can recall having lunch with a prominent minister in our nation. When I asked him how his church was going he gave me the standard ministerial put-off: 'Everything is great!'

Yet I knew he was under it. His staff had let me know.

I then mentioned how I had just come through a difficult patch. He looked at me and said, 'Let me be honest with you …' And he poured out his struggles and challenges. The accountability came as a result of me being vulnerable.

GROWING BIG PEOPLE

Establishing direction and significance, with their benefits of loyalty, strength, trust and accountability, are part of building the people you lead. Henry Ford once said, 'You can take my factories, burn up my buildings, but give me my people and they will bring my business right back again.' *People* bring growth – not structure, buildings or even business plans.

The role of the leader is to grow big people. The development of people is the key.

Big People Need Encouragement
Encouragement is the fuel that inspires people's sense

of self-importance. Positive reinforcement is absolutely essential to make people feel significant. Everybody loves encouragement. Do it privately, do it publicly, just do it! This will keep them strong in feelings of value. In turn, they will be an asset both to you as a leader and to the organisation as a whole.

Encourage people to act on their dreams. It is important to keep the big picture in mind, the whole horizon in focus. Often people get caught up in the little glitches, the mundane or the task at hand, without stepping back to see the enormity of what they are doing.

> *A leader needs to know the desires and dreams of the people*

Four keys to encouragement

1. *Give verbal encouragement.*
2. *Reward for effort.*
3. *Praise in front of peers.*
4. *Be thankful for their input and abilities.*

In our organisation, though my staff function in many different tasks for hours every day, we always keep the big picture in focus. Recently we gathered for a pre-production meeting before a major event. I began by playing a song we would use on the night.

Immediately everyone caught the big picture. I told them, 'At this point a singer will do this. At the end of the song we'll have the audience hold up banners. Then we'll get the crowd involved by doing this.' They could see how the song worked; they could see the response we would get from the thousands of people present. They stepped back from a task and saw the big picture.

In this way they gained a sense of what it would be like to be at the event, even though it was months away. They could see the end result and were encouraged to pursue it.

Dreaming the big picture added to their sense of significance, and it spurred them on.

Big People Want Support

In any organisation, people must have a system of support. They require all kinds of support: equipment support, skills support, support in family situations, support to believe in their vision and their dream.

One of the forgotten gifts of great leaders is to provide people with a sense of support, especially in a team environment. Make sure as a leader you give support.

Three elements of support

1. *Peer support* – Allow their peers and others to be supportive.
2. *Resource support* – Give them everything they need to do the job.
3. *Emotional support* – Give them your heart, ears and emotions.

As I share with many business and community leaders, I find the most difficult problems they face are not related to **cash-flow** or career path. They are problems associated with family, health, marriage – the day-to-day crises which assail them. Leaders must give emotional support. You don't have to be involved in every detail of people's lives, but a strong leader listens and supports.

Big People Have Initiative

Leaders release people to initiate. In most organisations – teams, businesses, churches, whatever – people are often afraid to initiate. They are stifled in their productivity. But I love initiative. I love people to take leadership and to do things which require thought and creativity.

If you want people to follow, you must ensure that your leadership style does not smother their initiative. Don't be threatened by initiative; rather, build on it. A threatened leader cannot lead, and a threatened ego is a sure recipe for others to avoid following you.

Leaders must trust that people are capable of doing what is required of them

Initiative and Boundaries

Recently, I spoke to a group of people and asked them what they felt a leader could do to encourage initiative. Many of them said a leader could *set boundaries* and let them know how far they could go on their own.

Interestingly, we discussed how boundaries do not

so much restrict as launch people out and release initiative. They give freedom to act without overstepping the mark. This is important.

People gain confidence to initiate through experience, time and constant encouragement

However, the leader must set the boundaries. Where no boundary is set, followers can't know when they have gone too far. Boundaries must be clear.

Another issue raised by my group was the importance of a leader not suppressing followers or standing over their shoulders. This is where trust comes in.

Where Does Initiative Originate?

Initiative arises when people feel familiar with their task. People gain confidence to initiate through experience, time and constant encouragement.

Initiative also flourishes when people take *ownership*. People like to use initiative forcefully, not aggressively, but in a precise way, knowing beforehand what the outcome will be. It is important to allow ownership and to encourage responsibility in those who follow.

We must understand that people rise to the occasion when it is their occasion. They rise to the challenge when it is their challenge. It is risky to transfer ownership of actions to the people who should be responsible, and it can be frightening. But it is imperative for people to understand that they are responsible if they are to own the task.

Great leaders desire to share their leadership. However, this requires a leader to release others for ownership and responsibility. It means negotiation, not dictatorship. When people are allowed to have input into decision-making, vision and direction, it encourages them to take ownership and be responsible for what they are doing. That in turn releases initiative.

Initiative in Shared Leadership

Occasionally a leader will hear things he doesn't really want to hear but needs to hear. A fearful follower will almost always tell a dictatorial leader what he or she wants to hear. A committed follower will take the initiative and say what is imperative for the leader to hear.

The rule of thumb when you ask for feedback is: Don't shoot the messenger.

> *The rule of thumb when you ask for feedback is: Don't shoot the messenger*

Leaders who want to develop other leaders through relationship must allow people to have input into the life of their organisation. This develops the 'us' and 'we' mentality of an organisation. When people take ownership and responsibility, they become 'carriers' of the organisation. In other words, they don't work for it – they carry it inside them.

Sharing Ownership of the Vision

Peter Drucker, an influential leadership writer, once

stated, 'No executive has ever suffered because his people were strong and effective.' You will be more effective when people take ownership of your vision.

A brilliant book, *Flight of the Buffalo*, vividly portrays this principle. It compares the mentality of buffalo and geese.

Buffalo do exactly what the head buffalo tells them. Committed to one leader, buffalo stand around motionless until the chief shows them what to do. When the leader is not around they wait for him to show up. Early settlers in America decimated entire buffalo herds by killing the lead buffalo, leaving the rest without direction and, therefore, easy prey.

When we have a mentality of single ownership, people are not decisive and action-oriented. Instead they are waiting for the next set of instructions and rules to come down from the top.

In contrast, when geese fly in their 'V' formation, the leader changes frequently. Different geese, at different times, initiate the lead. Each goose is responsible for getting the group where it needs to go. It changes its function or role whenever it is necessary, alternating between leading and following, following and leading. When the tasks change, the geese are responsible for changing the structure.

This is a living illustration of the principle of shared leadership. It works.

John Maxwell in *Developing the Leaders Around You* mentions more about geese:

When you see geese heading south for the winter

flying along in a 'V' formation, you might be interested in knowing that science has discovered why they fly that way. Research has revealed that as each bird flaps its wings, it creates an uplift for the bird immediately behind it. By flying in a 'V' formation, the whole flock adds at least 71% greater flying range than if each bird flew on its own.

Whenever a goose falls out of formation, it suddenly feels the drag and resistance of trying to go it alone. It quickly gets back into formation to take advantage of the lifting power of the bird immediately in front. When the lead goose gets tired, he rotates back in the 'V' and another goose flies the point. The geese honk from behind to encourage those up front to keep up their speed. And finally, when a goose gets sick, or is wounded by gunfire and falls out, two other geese fall out of formation and follow it down to help and protect it. They stay with the goose until it is either able to fly again or is dead, and then they launch out on their own or with another formation to catch up with their group.

Whoever was the first to call another person a 'silly goose' didn't know enough about geese.

There's a lot to learn from geese:

- People who have a common direction and sense of community get where they are going more quickly and easily because they are travelling on one another's slip stream.
- If we have as much sense as a goose

we will stay in formation, and so will those who are headed the same way we are.

- It pays to take turns doing hard jobs.
- When you honk from behind, make sure it's encouraging.
- If we have the sense of a goose, we will stand by each other as they do.

Encouraging Initiative and Ownership

If you want to successfully encourage ownership in your followers, do the following:

- Tell them it's theirs.
- Show them why it's theirs.
- Encourage their input into the vision.
- Let them be a sounding board, not just an echo.
- Develop the 'us' and 'we' mentality.
- Allow for the implementation of others' ideas.
- Avoid being a Mr or Mrs Fix-it – let others be responsible, too.
- Let them be responsible for monitoring their own performance.
- Celebrate victories with them.

'Example is not the main thing in influencing others, it's the only thing.'
Albert Schweitzer

The last and most important tip is this: *Change your leadership style to create a leadership theme.* You must be an example of the leadership style you require from your people.

Albert Schweitzer once said, 'Example is not the main thing in influencing others, it's the only thing.' If you want others to take ownership, you must take ownership yourself *and* allow for others to take ownership. They in turn will help others to take ownership.

The key to such leadership is mentoring, a subject to which we shall now turn our attention.

CHAPTER TWO

THE LEADER AS A MENTOR

The greatest need of both our generation and future generations is that of mentoring. Mentoring is the means by which we not only affect the present but the future, too. The lack of mentors forces future leadership onto shaky ground. Only solid mentoring produces big people, and building big people is what it takes for businesses and organisations to succeed and grow.

Mentoring is all about growing big people, first by being mentored and becoming a bigger person yourself (which never stops, because you're never too old or too qualified to learn from others), and then by mentoring others and passing on what you can. Mentoring is all about becoming greater than we presently are, through benefiting from, and benefiting, others. It's about mentors seeking followers and 'mentorees' seeking leaders, and it's about all of us becoming bigger and better than we are today.

In this chapter I will discuss the importance of building followers through mentoring.

WHAT IS MENTORING?

Mentoring can be likened to taking something old and something new and putting the two together. At thirteen years of age, Michelangelo was assigned as apprentice to the painter Domenico Ghirlandaio. From the master Michelangelo learned techniques that he would later use in painting the Vatican's beautiful Sistine Chapel. Such master/apprentice relationships go all the way back to the ancient days of Babylon and even earlier. They were a guarantee that there would be enough craftsman available to fulfil the needs of the community.

Mentoring is the means by which we not only affect the present but the future, too

In biblical times, too, one can see how a young Joshua learned by following Moses; how Ruth was adopted by the people of Naomi; how Paul made a disciple of Timothy. Each one of these young proteges went on to become marvellous men and women of history in their own right through the mentoring process. Mentoring truly is embarking on a journey to greatness. Sometimes that journey takes unexpected paths.

Retired businessman Fred Smith wrote a book called *You and Your Network*. I have a habit of reading it over and over again. Fred wanted to sing in a metropolitan opera company. One day an older friend said to him, 'Fred, you have everything except talent, and without that, all the practice, discipline and hope will not accomplish what you want. So, I suggest you find another field.' Although these words were painful, he listened and changed his direction into business. That's where he blossomed. A mentor was willing to be honest and yet cheer him on.

It's the mentor who is there to hug, to love and to ask how the protege is doing. It's the mentor who provides a sense of belonging and identity, and who affirms their gifts and allows them permission to go and be themselves. Mentoring is vital because it satisfies the longings of both the protege and the mentor.

Mentoring Begins with Me

I often say to people, 'Show me who your compasses in life have been!' Your *compasses* (your mental, emotional and character guides) and your *acquaintances* (those with whom you keep company) give a fair assessment of what kind of person you are now and will ultimately become. After all, iron sharpens iron, but lead will sink you quickly to the bottom.

There comes a time in our lives when all of us must ask who has helped us to become the person we are today. Who has helped to make or fashion you? Who are the people who have come into your life and influenced you profoundly? Who has 'marked' you permanently?

Such influence can, of course, be either positive or negative. But whether for good or for ill, all of these people have been your mentors.

As a young student in college, I can remember being totally captivated by the gifts of one of my lecturers. He was an incredible speaker, and I longed to get in the car and to drive him from meeting to meeting. I can honestly say that one of the key influences on my life was this particular gentleman. I knew that if we

Iron sharpens iron, but lead will sink you quickly to the bottom

brought people to his meetings their lives would be changed. I had the great privilege to watch as he moved an audience with his eloquence and passion. He became one of my mentors in life.

Earlier, my guitar teacher had been my mentor, encouraging me continually. I was always keen on being an up-front, on-stage person, and in my first years of learning the guitar I entered mime competitions mimicking other people's music. Although it sounds very corny, it was my guitar teacher who kept encouraging me to excel in performance on the public platform. This has impacted me for life.

People such as these – people who have shaped my

life and your life – are called mentors. I want to ask you, though: Who will shape the lives of people in generations to come? Who will be the moulders of a new generation of people in fields such as business, economics, law, ethics, the church and community life? Without mentors we face a very bleak future.

The truth is, *mentoring begins with me*. I have had my own mentors, so I must also become a mentor.

Why Mentoring is Important

Many people do not understand the importance of mentoring, but its benefits are great. Mentoring affects both the mentor and the mentoree. There is a sense of significance which happens; there is also a sense of bonding which will last a long time. Such bonding causes both people to find significance in each other.

'The high destiny of an individual is to serve rather than to rule'

Albert Einstein

I have been both a mentor and a mentoree, so I know the experience from both sides. For a mentor, there are few things more gratifying or pleasurable than seeing your mentoree succeed. It's one of the greatest feelings one can have and gives a true sense of fulfilment.

On the other hand, I often think about the men and women who have impacted my life, people who have taken the time to mentor me. It gives me a sense of great achievement to realise both that I can call them friends and that, in some small way, I have perhaps contributed to their lives as well.

To help get a picture of why mentoring is so important, let's change perspective for a moment and look at things from the mentoree's point of view. Here's what good mentoring does for you:

Mentoring expands and creates growth in you

Mentors help you to grow and keep growing. Mentors develop you socially, mentally, physically and practically; in short, they increase your effectiveness as a person. They hold you accountable for your gifts and your potential. As such, mentors care more about what you *might* be than what you *are*.

Mentors provide a model to follow

For most of us, our lifestyle, leadership, dreams of success, values, home life, actions, businesses and habits are all modelled for us by others. All humans imitate and follow example, even when they don't want to do so.

Non-verbal communication is extremely powerful. There is a witty old saying that goes, 'Practise what

'There are no problems we cannot solve together, and very few that we can solve by ourselves'

Lyndon Baines Johnson

you preach.' In other words, don't *tell* me what you know or believe, *show* me! We feel this way because of the tremendous power of modelling and imaging.

There is another old saying which dovetails here: 'I can't hear what you're saying because your actions speak louder than your words.' We use these sayings to define hypocrisy and double-standards, but the very fact that we have them proves our intense longing to observe and follow patterns. It is imperative for us to have role models ourselves and to be role models for others.

Mentors help you reach your goals

Most people are not self-motivated. I would argue that all of us need someone to coach us and to stretch us further from time to time. It is amazing what a little encouragement can do for people. It helps them to go further than they would normally go and to achieve more than they could ever dream possible.

Mentors help you to influence other people

Howard Hendricks has written: 'At times, our influence will go unnoticed. It should be noticed. Anyone who is in any kind of leadership position will influence other people. This deserves to be recognised.' Mentors influence others, including you. Consequently, as a mentor yourself, you will influence others.

Mentoring as a Process

Mentoring is, first of all, a process. It comes about when an individual who knows the ropes of a particular enterprise is willing to teach them to someone else. It is not exclusively a male thing; it's something women can do, too. Every one of us can be a mentor to someone else by instilling into their lives, our own values, skills and abilities. We mentor when we create opportunities for them they otherwise would not have.

In 1919, a young man recovering from terrible injuries suffered in the Great War in Europe rented an apartment in Chicago. He decided to live close to the house of Sherwood Anderson, the famous author, who had written a highly acclaimed collection of short stories entitled *Winsburg, Ohio*.

Anderson had a unique trait in that he was willing to help young writers. The two men became very close friends – they shared meals, walked together and discussed writing and creativity. The younger man often

> *'The deepest principle of human nature is the craving to be appreciated'*
> **William James**

bought samples of his work to Anderson, who at times responded with some very strong critiques. However, the young writer never lost his enthusiasm. Each time he would listen and take notes and then go back and improve his material. He opted to listen to instruction. He didn't suffer from the insecurity of continuously trying to defend himself. Later he said, 'I didn't know how to write until I met Sherwood Anderson.' One of the most helpful things Anderson did for his young protege was to introduce him to his network of associates in the publishing world.

In 1926, this same young man published his first

novel which met with immediate and great acclaim, *The Sun Also Rises*. His name was Ernest Hemingway.

But the story goes on. After Hemingway left Chicago and moved to New Orleans, Anderson met another young man, a poet, with a great desire to improve his skills. Anderson put him through the same routine and paces as Hemingway, writing, discussion, encouragement, critique and challenge. He gave the young man copies of his own writings and encouraged him to read them: their words, their themes, their development of characters. A year later Anderson helped the young man publish his first novel, *Soldier Pay*. Three years later, the bright new talent, William Faulkner, produced *The Sound and the Fury*, and it became an American masterpiece. A famous literary critic, Malcolm Cowley, said Anderson was 'The only writer of his generation to leave a mark on the style and vision of the next generation.'

> ### 'Always do more than is required of you'
> **General George S. Patton**

My question to you as a leader is: *What will you pass on to the next generation?* You don't have to be old or a writer to be a mentor. All you need is a vision for your own influence to increase far beyond seventy or eighty years of this life. A mentor leaves a legacy which others will follow and reproduce, and that legacy is the process of mentoring.

The Office of Mentor

The business world desperately needs mentors to encourage men and women to live the kind of lives that will bring success. Do not be threatened by young up-and-comers. Rather, train them and teach them.

(By the way, this may mean mentoring someone your own age through your own business, introducing them to new opportunities and giving them aid when they need it. Allow them to bounce their own concepts and ideas off you for your scrutiny and input. Remember, there is a process going on.)

Mentoring is fathering, mothering – whatever you want to call it. It's not the title that matters; it's the *process* of mentoring which needs to happen. Mentoring is a lot more than a matter of transferring data; it means coming alongside someone and guiding them in their much-needed personal and professional development.

> *Mentoring is a lot more than a matter of transferring data*

Mentoring helps people grow into maturity and into their full potential. It doesn't happen through a course or a program; it happens through relationship.

Mentoring as Relationship

Sometimes on my overseas speaking trips, I organise one of the interns of our organisation to travel with me. Not only do I get to spend quality time with that person, but they also get to feel the hectic pace on the road.

Recently one of my interns came with me on a trip to the USA where I was speaking at one of the largest music festivals in the country. He was as happy as a pig in mud. He got to appear on TV with me – I never lived that one down! He got to meet some of the world's top music artists.

'It takes a great man to make a good listener'

Sir Arthur Helps

Ben also learned that there are some things in life you can't ignore. Here's what happened.

We were in Hawaii speaking in a church and we went out to have some recreational time on a wave-runner. Then we had to quickly catch a flight from Honolulu to Harrisburg. Ben didn't have time to dry his clothes so he packed them wet in his suitcase. It's a long flight from Honolulu to Harrisburg, and to make matters even more precarious, we had a 24-hour stop in Pittsburgh. When we finally arrived in our small hotel room and Ben opened his case, the unbelievable odour made me gag.

Having not dried his clothes, Ben had then proceeded to forget about them. As his mentor it was my duty to inform my young protege that, when one is sharing a very small room, the smell of damp clothes is not conducive to building strong relationships. Ben learned a couple of things and I was more than willing to teach him. The first was that washing and drying of clothes is mandatory on the road. The other was that I'm very good on arranging funerals!

Seriously, though, in the office of mentor there is often plenty of dirty work to do. It comes with the territory, because relationships don't come easy.

The Relational Leader

Relationship is a theme I will reiterate again and again in this book. You can't be a leader if you don't want to reproduce yourself in your followers, and you can't reproduce yourself without building quality connections with people. Mentoring is all about these relational connections. Peter Drucker describes four simple and powerful qualities that are true of quality leadership and therefore of quality mentoring:

1. *Leaders are defined by followers.* This means leaders must be mentors.
2. *An effective leader is not someone who is loved or admired, but someone whose followers do the right things.* Popularity is not leadership; results are. Mentoring is all about reproducing your values in others.
3. *Leaders are highly visible; they set examples.* Mentors are living examples.
4. *Leadership is not rank, privileges, titles, or money, it is responsibility.* Mentoring is not all fun and games; it is serious work.

Getting to Know People

Mentoring is speaking into the lives of people through relationships. Relational leaders understand this, and within their business, community, church and civic life they seek to build relationships which enable them to impart their knowledge and experience to others. Some things can't be learned from books. Some things develop out of one-to-one contact with people.

Mentoring requires getting to know people, not necessarily know more about people. It is about knowing *why* they do what they do and making time to grow in your understanding of them. Today, we are desperate for people to believe in us, stand by us, guide us, teach us, encourage us and offer us accountability. We need their smiles, their hugs, their frowns, their correction, their tears, their pats on the shoulder, their arms around us, their constructive rebuke.

We need it all. It's all a part of mentoring. The leader who wants to mentor properly must build relationships.

MENTORING – HOW TO

How Mentoring Begins

So far I've discussed what mentoring is and why it's so important. But how do you go about it? It begins with your attitude as a mentor.

1. Mentoring begins with *a genuine concern about someone*. When you are together with your protege, the conversation and time spent is not considered a waste. He or she might be too young to be your peer, but you would nonetheless like to duplicate yourself in them. On the other hand, mentors do

not necessarily need to be older than their protégés. Even in our own work, I have found that sometimes the mentors, particularly with youth, are not that much older than the young people they guide. They become role models who both understand and provide a sense of belonging to people who desperately need to be taught.

Mentoring begins with a commitment to your own personal growth

2. Mentoring begins with *a commitment to your own personal growth*. Being a mentor helps you stay connected with yourself, both to monitor your own growth and to challenge yourself to sharpen mental, spiritual and emotional skills.

3. Mentoring begins with *a desire to be open*. This will include being able to share your own strengths and weaknesses.

4. Mentoring begins with *a decision to both affirm and call to account*. This means you will encourage your mentoree and also to correct them.

5. Mentoring begins with *a will to live out what you say*. This is not perfection; it's integrity – practising what you preach.

So, that's how mentoring begins. How does it continue? How do you actually go about mentoring people? I've been in the mentoring business for years, so let me give you some advice from my own stock of wisdom.

Take the Initiative

First, *always take the initiative*. Find someone who is keen and hungry for a mentor. You must be pro-active. Don't take the attitude, 'They can come looking for me if they want me.' 'They' probably never will.

Once you take the initiative to be a mentor, your first job is to find someone with that steely glint in their eye, who looks

We will identify the future in other people

like they want to grow. You may see it in their eagerness, their teachability, their open heart, their zeal, their willingness to respond or serve. Watch for the person who continually asks questions – that's the kind of person you're looking for.

Here specifically is what to look for in a mentoree:

1. *Look for someone with hunger* – a person who refuses to drift in life. Mentors want to work with someone who is heading somewhere and who isn't just interested in a quick pep talk. A mentoree must want to achieve, learn and develop.

2. *Look for someone willing to take responsibility and fulfil given tasks and assignments*. The best mentors and mentorees are those who want to increase their capacities.

3. *Look for initiative*. Mentors want someone who doesn't wait for others to do everything for them – someone who is willing to grab opportunities, seize the day, run hard.

4. *Look for an eager learner.* Is there someone already listening to tapes, already reading books, already trying to develop themselves? They are probably ripe for mentoring.

5. *Look for a willingness to assume personal responsibility for growth, action and consequences.* Mentors want someone who is not going to pass the buck, but who is willing to take the consequences of failure as readily as celebration and praise.

Make Your Intentions Clear

Second, once you find this person, *make your intentions clear.* Tell them what you want to achieve.

You may be saying, 'Well, why don't they come to me? Why do I need to chase them?' The answer is simple: many potential proteges are intimidated by successful people. Most people are scared to ask for help. They are afraid of rejection, afraid of being looked down upon, afraid of not being accepted. Sometimes, they don't even realise the latent potential within them. There's nothing odd about that.

Most people saw a big chunk of marble, but Michelangelo saw David

For someone to come along and extend an arm of acceptance and friendship is a tremendous step forward. As a leader you must go to them, and after that initial contact, I can guarantee that they will come back looking for you. Many powerful people once thought they didn't have anything to offer.

There was once a time when they too were without training or skill.

Leaders need to have eyes like Michelangelo. Most people saw a big chunk of marble, but Michelangelo saw David – and the rest, as they say, is history.

What should you say to the person you wish to mentor? They have many natural fears and concerns, but since you have substantially more experience in life, you must reach out to make an input to their lives. I guarantee it will not only help you become a more successful person, but it will permit you to leave a legacy – one that will be talked about for ages to come.

Be Available

Third, *make yourself available* to people. Even though successful leaders have hectic schedules, their time, as little or as much as can be given, is a major investment in the lives of others; they will appreciate it. The most precious commodity is time, and the best asset you have is your people. Put the two together and you have a great recipe for success.

The best asset you have is your people

Make yourself available to spend time on grooming them. Influence will arise out of relationship; it surely never arises from a manual or a lecture.

You don't necessarily need to be an incredible communicator to be a good mentor – just someone who shares from the heart.

One of the young guys who works diligently in my intern program always brings a pen and paper to write down a thought, idea or saying. He's hungry to learn and I'm hungry to teach him. I know it requires time, but it's worth it.

But how can we add this burden to our already hectic schedules? I suggest that we may need to be more efficient with our time *and* our relationships. For example, I am always on planes, flying here, there and everywhere. So, I try to have one of my team, an intern or one of our young men, drive me to the airport. During that trip we can talk for an hour and spend time discussing our dreams, plans and visions. During lunchbreaks, too, we can make the most of encouraging people. You don't have to eat alone.

Don't just share the things you have in common; share your dreams, your personal goals, your successes *and* your failures! You don't even need to have an agenda. Neither do you need to be an expert at everything. To be a mentor you simply need to be interested. Just hang out and share honestly.

Creating Lasting Opportunities

Very often, when I am visiting and speaking on some of our programs in high schools, I ask the leaders in the area to introduce me to their young Turks, the ones trying to establish themselves as workers communicating with young people in high schools. I take them with me in the car. They drive me around and we talk. I ask them questions about their dreams and aspirations. Often they ask me about the keys to success and the lessons

I have gleaned in my years of working with youth or speaking to the business world. I share a few home truths, the sort of things you can't always get out of a textbook. They come from personal experience. They are things to be caught, not taught.

A few years ago, I was speaking at a camp at the request of a youth leader friend, Phil. He shared with me his concern about one particular young man in his youth group, Ross. Apparently, Ross was always looking to be the centre of attention. His mischievous personality was always getting him and his friends into trouble. Phil's attitude was 'He's a rebel.'

However, when I met Ross I liked him. He had personality and charisma. He and I became quite good friends at camp. I said to Phil, 'There's nothing wrong with Ross. He's a leader and has a great desire to help other people, even if it is misdirected at times. He could be your greatest asset.'

Unfortunately, Phil didn't take my advice. Today, he is doing nothing and his youth group is depleted. Ross, however, was mentored by someone else, and became first the leader of one of the largest youth groups in the country, then Associate *Your worst night-* Minister at one of the largest *mare is probably* churches in the country, and *your best asset* finally leader of his own thriving congregation.

Make yourself available! Your worst nightmare is probably your best asset.

A Career in Modelling?

Fourth, *take up a career in modelling*. In other words, model your life for others. People can forget what we say, but they will never forget what we do. The behaviour you model for others will be followed.

As a Youth Pastor, I did something once that taught me a great lesson. One day I changed out of my jeans and t-shirt into a tie and shirt with a collar. My wife, totally bewildered, said to me, 'What are you doing?' I replied, 'Watch.'

For the next few weeks I kept wearing a shirt and tie. After about the fourth week I noticed all the young guys in the youth group wearing shirts and ties. After they had done that for a few weeks, I went back to a t-shirt and jeans.

By now my wife knew exactly what I was up to. I was trying to teach a lesson to some of my leaders: people will follow what you do more than what you say. Not long after my reversion to t- shirts and jeans, the young men in the youth group began to wear jeans and t-shirts, too. They were simply playing 'follow the leader.' Clearly, I had a career in modelling to rival Elle MacPherson's!

Be a Role Model

Anyone who wants to be mentor will be a role model in all areas of life. Isn't it amazing that you can watch a TV program, see one of the actors slam a door during a fight, and do the very same thing yourself when you next have an argument? TV has modelled behaviour for you, and you have imitated. A mentor will always be an

Anyone who wants example of appropriate behav-
to be a mentor will iour. You can model family
relationships – rearing happy
be a role model in children; *communication* –
all areas of life being a good listener; *love* –
treating your spouse correct-
ly; *how to dress; how to speak; what to read, how to work
or study.* Are you allowing anyone the precious opportunity of sharing your experience in life?

Marks of a Quality Mentor
Having established the framework for a mentoring relationship, let's consider certain key qualities you need to
develop as a relational leader who wants to be a good
mentor. I'll list them here, and then we can examine
them one by one.

- Be accessible.
- Give wise counsel.
- Give due recognition.
- Reprimand as needed.
- Discipline if and when necessary.

Be Accessible
I've already discussed this under the heading 'Be
Available', but it bears repeating. You can't build walls
to shut out those you wish to lead. A leader must be
accessible to followers. And accessibility means to
have an openness where what needs to be said can be
said.

Of course, you must also avoid being 'one of the boys.' If you get too familiar with your followers, your input into their lives may be diluted. You can be a friend, but you are *still* the leader and mentor.

Give Wise Counsel

Some of the most powerful and intimate times between mentors and followers are those one-to-one meetings when you can honestly confront the good, bad, indifferent, productive and non-productive. This is where a leader can discover the things that bother followers. It is also the place to answer their questions and to deal with unresolved conflicts or frustration over difficulties.

My suggestion is that mentors should offer counsel under the following circumstances:

- Whenever it's required.
- If performance is slipping.
- When creative input and advice is needed.
- When the mentoree's future is being decided.
- When there are obvious relational or practical problems.
- When issues hinder them from fulfilling their true potential.

My strong advice is to make these times of counsel as casual as possible. However, don't allow the casual nature of the event to stifle the importance of either what is

Always offer practical suggestions on what to do

said or what needs to be done. Always offer practical suggestions on what to do. Write out specific goals and assist the person in developing targets; list improvements you would like to see made.

Give Due Recognition

It's very important to give people recognition and encouragement for jobs well done. Retired US army Major-General Albury 'Red' Newman, author of two books on leadership, has written: 'In command and leadership many qualities, attributes, and techniques are required including drive, force, judgement, perception, and others. But nothing can replace the inspiration and lift that comes from commending a job well done.' Give people as much recognition as possible, praising them, encouraging them and honouring them.

Reprimand as Needed

As a mentor you're not always going to be the good guy or the good girl. Sometimes you will need to offer discipline and strong direction.

Ken Blanchard and Spencer Johnson offer these words on discipline in their ground-breaking book, *The One Minute Manager:* 'Reprimand people immediately. Tell people what they did wrong. Be specific. Tell them how you feel about what they did wrong and in no uncertain terms.'

Discipline If and When Necessary

The meaning of the word discipline is 'to teach'. It's the

word for *'disciple*ship'. Discipline is not primarily punishment; it is there to restore, adjust and assist a person
so that they do not to fall into the mentality of a 'slack-
er.' Discipline exists to help people grow in the areas
where growth is desperately needed and where change
is a necessity.

BEING MENTORED

This chapter has concentrated so far on what it means to be a mentor, but there's another side to the mentoring relation-ship. What does mentoring look like from the viewpoint of the mentoree? You may be

Anyone who wants to grow as a leader must take inventory of the self and the inner life

saying, 'I don't feel like being a mentor. I'm the kind of
person who needs to be mentored.' And you're right! In
fact, *even mentors need to be mentored*!

I have mentors in my life. Often I will sit down with people who are very successful in business or other areas of
leadership and ask them to speak into my life. I ask them
to gauge my performance, to tell me where I can improve
and to show me how I can communicate better.
Sometimes they tell me things I don't want to hear.
They're the things I really need to hear. This kind of input
will always help me to grow and reach my full potential.

So here are a few words of advice for anyone who
wants to build a relationship with a mentor, starting
with how to choose an appropriate person.

What Sort of Mentor Do I Need?
Identify Your Needs

The first thing to do is to *find out what you need*. Most people say 'I want a mentor' but they don't know what it is they really need. It's vital, if you are serious about finding a mentor, to identify the skills, knowledge, attitudes or character you most want to develop. Then you can intelligently seek the kind of person who is best suited to help you.

Dr A.W. Tozer, a great preacher of the past, offered a series of questions to assist people in determining the kind of person they were: *What do you want most? What do you think about most? How do you use your money? What do you do with your leisure time? What is the company you keep? Whom and what do you admire? What do you laugh at?* To these I would add two further questions: *What do I want from life?* and *What stands between me and my desired goals, visions, dreams and ambitions?* All of these things can determine the kind of person you are, and consequently what kind of mentor you need.

> *There must be a hunger within you for teaching*

Another way to determine your needs is to take a personal inventory. Anyone who wants to grow as a leader must take an inventory of the self and the inner life. For myself, I do this every three to six months. I assess where I'm at, what I'm doing, my time commitments, the state of my marriage, the checks and balances I have instituted to pace myself, and my reading habits. I ask myself, 'Is all this appropriate, or am I getting in over my head?' I also ask myself where I need to improve in areas such as communication, relationships and my capacity as a father, husband and leader. What areas of my life do I need to change? What attitudes sneak up on me?

Are You Willing to Pay the Price?

The second element to consider when seeking a mentor is *what price are you willing to pay* to have a mentor? Are you serious about this or is it just a fanciful idea? There is a price to everything in life, and you must weigh up the cost carefully. You cannot go into mentoring half-heartedly: you are either in it or not. If you are in it, then pay the price required – whatever that is!

Are You Willing to Listen?

Third, in choosing a mentor ask yourself, *Am I willing to listen to this person who will mentor me?* There is no point getting mixed up with a mentor you don't respect or don't want to hear from. You must be willing to engage with your teacher fully.

Getting the Most from Being Mentored

Having found your mentor, what attitudes should you bring to the mentoring relationship?

Be Willing to Learn

First, there must be a hunger within you for teaching.

Too often, we think we know it all, have heard it all or seen it all. But are we doing all? That is the key question. You must be hungry to be a doer.

Create ways for yourself to get closer to the person whom you have chosen as mentor (or who has chosen you as a mentoree). When people come to me for counselling in various areas of their lives, I ask them the question: 'Have you tried any of the things that I suggested you do?' When the response is either, 'What things did you tell me to do?' or 'No, I didn't,' I know such people are neither hungry nor interested. They just want a quick fix to their problem.

Talent without humility is like a drunk at the wheel of a car - it's just an accident waiting to happen

So, if you are someone who wants to be mentored, learn first to *listen to*, then to *do* what your mentor teaches. Apply what you're learning. A mentor can't help anyone who isn't hungry or willing to apply what is taught. We can talk theories until the cows come home; we can talk around and around problems until we're blue in the face. But unless we take practical steps to ensure our success and growth, we will never be the people we were intended to be, no matter how good our mentor is.

Be Teachable
The second thing to do is closely related to the first and

requires a little humility. You must not only be hungry for teaching, but you must *be teachable.*

Having humility doesn't mean becoming a doormat. Humility stems from you being a secure person who knows and accepts yourself. Humility means that even if you have to do the hard yards and submit to someone's authority, you will still engage in the process.

When you're being mentored, keep your ears open, your eyes peeled and your mouth shut. Listen and learn.

Have the Right Attitude

Third, there's a wrong attitude to mentoring: 'I don't need this other person to teach me, I'm the best, the brightest, and most talented.' That's a recipe for failure. We need humility of heart toward our mentors if we are to grow.

I once heard a guy say, 'Talent without humility is like a drunk at the wheel of a car – it's just an accident waiting to happen.' The way to prevent such tragedy is to bring yourself under the guiding hands of a seasoned, mature individual whom you can emulate. It doesn't mean you ignore your gifts; it means you filter them through the eyes of someone who has seen a lot more than you.

Be Loyal

Fourth, loyalty is a key factor. If there is one indictment on Western society in general, it's that loyalty is a rare commodity. Loyalty when things get tough, loyalty

when you are tempted to get the better deal and cruci-
fy relationships. Loyalty is absolutely essential, crucial,
imperative – and any other power word you can think
of!

Mentoring is a two-way street. You place confidence
and trust in your mentor, and he or she places confidence and trust in you. That
means you must be able to
keep confidences when confidences are shared. The mentor has given you his time,
wisdom, experience, work,
network, associates, input,
family-life and sometimes the
innermost secrets of his or her own personal life. You
must never, ever betray that trust.

*How you handle
trust will determine
how much others
entrust you*

To do so is not only wrong; it is also a recipe for dis-
aster in your own life. Judas did not sell Jesus for thirty
pieces of silver – *he sold himself.* Loyalty demands you
be responsible with information. You must keep personal matters in your confidence. How you handle trust
will determine how much others will entrust to you.

One of the greatest Bible stories of loyalty is the story
of the life of Joseph. Joseph lived in the house of
Potiphar, a high official of the Egyptian Pharaoh.
Potiphar had so much wealth that he put it all under the
care of Joseph, a person whom he could trust to be
loyal. However, Potiphar's faithless wife 'got the hots'
for young Joseph and tried to draw him into an illicit
relationship. He ran from that situation and kept his loy-

alty intact. Joseph was one of that rare breed of men who know that it takes more than a zipper to make a man. Potiphar had put incredible trust in Joseph. Joseph proved himself trustworthy with the most important thing Potiphar had, his own wife.

If you are being mentored, make sure you remain loyal and trustworthy, and do not go over the boundaries that have been set in areas of trust and responsibility.

Crave Feedback

Being mentored means you need to ask, learn, follow up, and grow. Marshall Goldsmith wrote a brilliant essay on this very subject in his book *The Leader of the Future*. He says, 'The effective leader of the future will consistently ask to receive feedback and to solicit new ideas.' Years ago, people, especially leaders, were discouraged from seeking feedback. Today, however, the majority of the world's most highly respected leaders ask for 360-degree feedback.

Don't be afraid of feedback, welcome it positively

Leaders also need to learn and grow, and there are two keys to learning:

1. *Effective listening* and
2. *Reflection after asking for and receiving information.*

One author puts it this way, 'Asking for input and then shooting the messenger who delivers the bad news is worse than not asking at all.' So, don't be afraid of feedback; welcome it positively. Learning will often require follow-up; this means developing action plans, checking on progress, and getting further assistance.

Growth is the by-product. How does this happen? Through input, positive response, training and listening to your mentors. It's *getting in shape, staying in shape,* and *being in shape* for the tasks ahead.

KEYS TO SUCCESSFUL MENTORING

The responsibilities of the mentor are awesome ones, for they pertain to the growth and development of other people's lives. Therefore, there are many keys to successful mentoring

Leading from the Front

Probably the foremost key is *leading from the front.* Peter Drucker says in his book *Leader of the Future,* 'effective leaders were not preachers, they were doers.' Mentors, as effective relational leaders, cannot just lead from a desk; they must lead from the front.

Often in times of war, you hear of soldiers who are frustrated with the guys sitting behind office desks, firing off orders while the real battle is going on in the field. A mentor must know his field. Knowing

Leadership stands out in front and says 'Follow me'

your field means you have to be in there working the field, getting your hands dirty. That doesn't mean you do all the menial tasks, but it does mean being involved with people. You are cultivating them and they are your field.

John D. Rockefeller once said, 'I will pay more for the ability to deal with people than for any other ability under the sun.' Why is that? Because people bring growth; people cause productivity; people build organisations no matter what the structure.

In my work with youth, I could be an expert on youth culture, spending all my time reciting lyrics to the latest popular songs. But unless I'm out there feeling some of the pain the kids feel, I won't be able to speak to them with authority, passion or a sense of understanding.

Leaders on the field are admired because they can be mentors on the field; they can be duplicated precisely *because* they are on the field. They can lead by example and show others *because* they are on the field.

Being on the Field

On the field you work *with* people. Someone once remarked, 'One man working *with* you is worth a dozen men working *for* you.' As leaders it is so easy to hide behind desks, sending memos and doing the menial administrative tasks. But that's not leadership – it's management. Leadership stands out in front and says, 'Follow me.'

On the field you notice the achievements and hard work of others – and, instead of bragging about your-

A single arrow is easily broken but not in a bundle of ten

self, you can find time to brag about them. In this way you will excite them to even greater achievements. On the field you communicate with people and are able to apply things you've learned. It's where you forge powerful relationships and friendships, building trust and commitment.

On the field you build mutual support. The biblical book of Ecclesiastes says, 'Two are better than one, because they have a good return for their work. If one falls down, his friend can help him up.' On the field you build relationships with people, so that when they fall you can help them up – and vice versa.

On the field you help others to become both better people and more successful. It's where you learn the 100% principle: 'Find the one thing you agree on with another person and then give it 100% of your encouragement' (John Maxwell).

On the field you learn to get along with people, which as Theodore Roosevelt stated, is 'The most important single ingredient in the formula of success.' And it's where you learn to care for people. As John Maxwell so aptly states, 'People don't care how much you know until they know how much you care.'

So, be on the field to meet people, to enlist people, to train people, to have an input into people. It's where you learn not to use people to build a great work but to use your work to build great people. Leaders find followers on the field.

What Field?

What do I mean by 'the field'? I am referring to the place of doing. 'The field' is where we work together as a team. There is an old Japanese proverb that says, 'A single arrow is easily broken but not ten in a bundle.'

Everyone on my team has learned to be a worker on the field. From the secretaries to the musicians, from the writing people to the sound people, from the event coordinators to the counsellors, they are all on the field. Everyone of them has to learn to work on the field.

After our events I encourage all the people in my team to go and meet the kids and talk with them. It's out there, on the field, that we will find our future singers, musicians, dancers, leaders, workers. And it's out there, on the field, that my team find the motivation for doing what they do.

I want to produce leaders with thick hearts and thin heads, not leaders with thick heads and thin hearts. My desire is to produce leaders in all areas of life – people who will not just be interested in splitting hairs but in breaking the chains that hold people back from reaching their full potential in life. Where does that happen? *On the field.*

> *I want to produce leaders with thick hearts and thin heads, not leaders with thick heads and thin hearts.*

General Douglas MacArthur's views are known to every West Point cadet. They are written in stone on the main athletic building at Westpoint: 'On the fields of friendly strife are sown the seeds that, on other fields, on other days, will bear the fruits of victory.' On the field we learn teamwork, team spirit, interdependency, working in rank, the power of unity, cohesion and building morale. We learn to listen to the captain, to help someone when they're injured, to go the extra mile because we're a team. We learn to rejoice when someone scores a goal and to defend when we're attacked.

Being out there on the field causes you to see things not just as a commentator or spectator but as a competitor. In sports, when a commentator speaks it is one thing, and when a spectator speaks it really doesn't have much clarity; but when a player speaks you know you've got it first-hand. On the field you can develop pride as a team or an organisation – pride in what you do.

Growing Big People through Mentoring

Ultimately, mentoring is all about leading; and, as we discussed in the first chapter, leading is about growing big people, building them up, toughening them up, honing them and sending them out to win. As a mentor-leader here are some qualities you might look to foster in your followers:

- Being the fastest.
- Being the most efficient.
- Being thorough.
- Being creative.
- Being productive.
- Working the longest hours.

- Producing the best results.
- Getting a better return.
- Creating greater dreams in others.
- Being of significance to others.

In this chapter we've seen that without relationships, the mentoring which is so integral to strong, vibrant leadership cannot occur. In the next chapter I will go on to talk further about what it means to be an effective relational leader.

CHAPTER THREE

QUALITIES
OF AN EFFECTIVE LEADER

In the last chapter we observed that *effective relationships* are integral to the task of mentoring and developing the next generation of leaders. Now I want to examine some more marks of the effective leader – the characteristics and traits that make relational leaders successful in building big people.

The many qualities needed for effective relational leadership would take volumes to describe, but I wish to stress here the major ones. We can start with one of the most fundamental: Vision – the importance of thinking big.

THINKING BIG

A leader has to be a big thinker, stretching beyond his or her own limitations. Seeing the big picture is a constant priority for anyone who wishes to be a successful leader. Without big thinking we make very little progress. It is important to understand that each small step is the result of one big thought.

How we think is also important in developing the actions of an organisation. John F Kennedy said, 'Some men see things as they are and say 'why', I dream of things that never were and say 'why not'.'

> *It is important to understand that each small step is the result of one big thought*

The big thinking leader sees the future as better than the present. As a big thinker, you will see the positive where the negative dwells; you will see opportunity where other people see problems; you will see beauty in the midst of great ugliness; you will find answers when other people seek only to question; you will look for solutions where others point the finger of blame; you will see potential in other people they don't see themselves. These attitudes are at the core of thinking big.

Thinking Big Creates Purpose

Not many years ago, our end-of-year Youth Alive events were not as large as our early-year events. We were faced with the possibility of moving to a smaller venue and down-sizing our end-of-year activities. Every excuse was given – it's close to Christmas; students are studying for exams; people are busy.

I believed in my heart the problem was vision. So, rather than go backwards into a smaller building and down-size our events, I felt the answer was to make them bigger and better, and hence to *give ourselves a purpose.*

As you are probably aware, the year 2000 is the year when Sydney hosts the Olympics, and I saw this as a great opportunity. What if we began to rally young people together *now*, prior to the Olympics, holding mass rallies and reaching out to young people with the purpose of leading up to the Olympics?

That's the challenge we set ourselves. Now, at the rate we're going, by the time we get to the Olympics we will have already amassed crowds of 80-100,000 people; and rather than trying to do it in one hit in 2000, we will have progressively reached that goal. Those meetings have become the largest gatherings in our youth program rather than the smallest, with almost double the attendance of our other events!

Beyond Imagination to Faith

Another important by-product of this renewed vision has been to work with other organisations who previously seemed hostile to what we were doing. Our competitors became our colleagues. It was a common vision, a common goal and a common purpose which drew us together. It required big thinking.

A big thinker will capture a vision, put it into words and inspire people to rise up in faith to accomplish the mission. As the author of *Making a Difference* says, 'Vision in its most exalted form reaches even beyond the limits of imagination.'

A big thinker will be big in faith, too. A story is told of a kindergarten teacher who once asked a child what she was drawing. The child replied, 'I'm drawing a picture of God.' The teacher, with some doubt in her heart, said, 'But sweetheart, no one knows what God looks like.' The child's powerful, faith-full reply came back, 'They will in a minute.'

That's a big thinker – someone who's able both to think and to believe they can achieve what they set out to do.

Big thinkers have faith in people, faith in themselves, faith in their mission, and faith in their community. When you read the newspaper headlines or watch the news reports, it's very hard to find faith – there's too much negativity out there. I want to state emphatically: *You can believe in people, you can believe in dreams, and you can believe in the ability of human beings to accomplish great things.*

The faith of a big thinker becomes a catalyst for others to launch out into the deep

Even in the darkest hours – hours of struggle, difficulty, recession, violence, crime – the most brilliant lights shine. A big thinker understands this and will continue to have faith. The faith of a big thinker becomes a catalyst for others to launch into the deep. The leader who develops skills as a big thinker will direct followers toward positive and fruitful living. He or she will provide opportunities for them that will enhance their capabilities. Never underestimate the power of big thinker to make a difference in the world.

The Problem with Assumptions

Big thinkers understand wrong assumptions are at the centre of bad decisions, wrong relationships and malfunctioning systems and people. We must guard against ever building on assumptions. Always check and double check assumptions. After all, assumptions are just what they are called – *assumptions!*

One of the most tragic and horrific examples of the problem with assumptions is the Vietnam War. I have visited the Washington Memorial commemorating the 58,000 young American soldiers killed in combat in Vietnam. I couldn't help but be moved. Robert MacNamara's book about Vietnam, *In Retrospect,* is a lesson in the nightmares of leadership. The premise of the book is that many of the decisions which promoted the Vietnam conflict were based on wrong assumptions.

I remember watching a movie in which someone asked what happens when you *assume* too much. The reply was poignant: You make an ASS out of U and ME.

Tips on Becoming a Big Thinker
1. *Always look on the bright side of life.*
2. *Keep the big picture in focus.*

3. *When in doubt, only believe.*
4. *Understand that things are never as bad as they seem. (They may be worse, but never as bad! Always keep your sense of humour.)*
5. *Every day brings another opportunity.*
6. *Keep your vision simple.*
7. *Never base decisions on assumptions.*
8. *Don't look at how things were, always look at how they can be.*
9. *Build a think-tank of big thinkers.*
10. *Be a risk-taker and imagine what can be done if you just believe.*

CREATIVITY

Another vital quality of the effective leader is creativity. A leader who wants to build big people must be creative. Often we limit creativity to the arts, but creativity can be manifested in many ways. It's not limited to pursuits such as music, poetry and writing. Creativity can be demonstrated in any activity in *the way things are done*. There can be creativity in business, creativity in motivating people, creativity in enlisting good people, creativity in rewarding, creativity in the way we work.

The crux of all creativity is the courage to change

Creativity and Change
The crux of all creativity is the courage to change.

Conversely, change requires creativity. The two go hand in hand. In my previous book *Dreamers Never Sleep* I argued that the only constant in life is change.

Changes seen in the last few years are amazing and boggle the mind. The Internet, new technology, the means of transport and communication, the capacity of every individual to earn money their parents could only dream of, are all in sight. When you look at all this change, the crux has been creativity. Creative people motivate and inspire change.

Creative people do not fly solo, however; they need good people around them to implement the changes. But they do become the catalysts, the feeders, the inspiration behind change.

> *'More than anything leadership is about creating a new way of life... leaders must foster change.'*
>
> **Kouzes Posner**

Kouzes Posner, in his book *The Leadership Challenge,* states, 'More than anything else, leadership is about creating a new way of life and to do that, leaders must foster change, take risks, and accept the responsibility for making change happen.' I want you to notice two words there *creating* and *change*. All change is created. When you create something new it inevitably results in change.

One of my great joys in life is watching young people develop their creativity. In the past twelve years, we have been able to release some into the arts and to encourage others into platform activities such as public inspirational speaking. But to accommodate them we have had to make changes – organisational changes, changes in the way we view and approach things, changes in our motivations. All this change required creativity.

The Roots of Creativity

1. *Creativity stems from dissatisfaction with the status quo.*
2. *A thought or a seed is planted.*
3. *That seed is watered and should grow and become a plant.*
4. *A creative plan must be seen in light of the mission, purpose and significance of the big picture.*
5. *Enlisting the people to implement the created idea.*

How Do You Develop Creativity?

Not all of us have a creative temperament, but all of us can develop a creative mindset. You can do this in the following ways:

- Talk about ideas out loud with trusted people, helping them understand your thinking.
- Spend time with creative people. As I've remarked already in this book, 'iron sharpens iron.'
- Never settle down when things are at their peak; this will keep you thinking and being creative.
- Always be hungry to make things better. Don't

allow your organisation, business or life to fall
into the passionless realm of self-content.
Always be hungry for more.
- Develop think-tank sessions for creativity.
- Be decisive.

Creativity and Being Decisive

I cannot think of a greater waste of energy, talent and
resources than indecision. Until a decision is made
nothing eventuates. The leader who makes decisions
knows that when issues are not faced, problems will last
forever.

Dilemmas are not resolved and solutions are not
found simply by churning problems over and over.
Anguished decisions can keep you up at night and
cause you to sweat over the various possible outcomes,
but at some point decisions must be made before any
action can be taken. And someone must take the
responsibility for those decisions. The hallmark of great
leadership is to make decisions in times of crisis and to
take the responsibility for these decisions. Indecision
holds up progress, stifles the future, thwarts financial
prosperity and cripples opportunity.

Until a decision is made, nothing eventuates. Indecision holds up progress, stifles the future, thwarts financial prosperity and cripples opportunity

The Danger of Procrastination and Indecision

Procrastination will not lead you into destiny or build the lives of people around you. I have often said that the greatest ability a human being has is the ability to decide. But the greatest inability a human being has is the inability to decide. Both have powerful consequences.

It's interesting that over and over again in the Scriptures we find that God challenges people to choose – to choose between life and death, blessing and cursing, prosperity and poverty, favour and failure.

Destinies can never be built on procrastination

Often procrastination and indecision come under the guise of 'let's set up a committee' or 'let's come back to it later on' or 'let's do a survey.' Although such strategies may be legitimate on occasion, very often they become excuses and cover-ups for indecision.

When I speak to young people I bring them to a point of decision in life. They can't go forward unless they decide to do so; they cannot give up drugs unless they decide to do so; they cannot seek better opportunities for their futures unless they decide to do so. *There can never be opportunity unless a decision is made.* There can never be prosperity unless a decision is made.

Destinies can never be built on procrastination. It spells death to an organisation and to people's future. It is a luxury effective leaders do not have.

Owning Decisions

As a leader you must not only make decisions; you must *stick with them*. Leaders who continually vacillate between decisions and retractions create only confusion, discouragement and disillusionment for an organisation.

Effective leaders *own* their decisions. They will be firm on a decision, and if they make a wrong decision they will be quick to answer and admit their mistake. Then they will make a decision to go on from there and not dwell on the mistake. It's all a matter of decisions.

Effective leaders own their decisions

People appreciate leaders who, when making wrong decisions, admit that they have done so. It takes guts to say these three words, 'I was wrong' – but it also requires a great leader to keep a level head when people say 'You were right.'

It's important to understand that leaders will sometimes make decisions on their own and sometimes after consultation. But if a leader makes all decisions yet later claims that the team or group made them, such a leader will lack credibility and honesty.

If you make decisions without consulting others, say so; if the team is expected to be involved, let them be involved. Let them know the expectations and procedures. Be honest about the decisions you make. If you say it's a team decision, make it a team decision. If it's your decision, make it yours. Either way is fine, but set the boundaries with statements that are clear and honest.

It's important to understand, of course, that committees and boards can often kill the decision-making process. J. Donald Walters writes, 'To many people, unfortunately, discussion is virtually a substitute for activity. They imagine that to say anything is tantamount to accomplishment.' The effective leader knows that an encyclopedia of good ideas is no substitute for even the least of them actually being put into practice.

It is good to encourage others to make decisions on their own. By doing so you build trust in them and they will grow in confidence. But make sure you understand that decisions will have multiple consequences and effects. It's important to make the right decisions, especially when they involve people.

Decisions – How to

In approaching decisions, ask yourself the following questions:

1. *Am I the right person to make this decision?* This doesn't mean that you pass the buck, but that you honestly assess if you are capable of making the decision. Are you too emotionally involved or emotionally uninvolved? Is the situation one about which you are well informed?

2. *Is the objective of the .decision clear?* In other words, is what I want to achieve clear enough in my own mind to make a decision?

3. *Am I acting or reacting?* Am I acting on a basis of the betterment of others, the betterment of my

organisation, or the future success of my own life? Or am I re-acting in anger and raw emotion?

4. *Have I considered all options?* Have I asked myself the 'for' and 'against' questions? Do I have the game plan to follow through on my decision? Do I need to consult with a team or a group in making my decision? A good decision-maker requires a sense of judgment, and judgment is a simple choice between different options.

There is nothing creative about avoiding decisions. One of the great lessons to learn in life is that, as leaders make good decisions, they develop better judgment and even more creativity. Good judgment is born out of experience. The leader with creativity and flair is a decision-maker, and people want wise judgments and decisions.

RISKY BUSINESS

The relational leader not only makes creative decisions, but he or she is also a risk-taker. *Learn to be a risk taker.* Paul Fulton, the former president of Sarah Lee, says this: 'Risk and confidence are the two characteristics that make ordinary managers into corporate entrepreneurs.' An effective leader will be a risk-taker and will work with risk-takers. If you fire or dump someone after they've made one mistake you really don't have the heart of a leader. You create fearful managers rather than develop courageous leaders. You must take a calculated gamble with people.

Risk is something we experience every day without even thinking about it. When you cross the street, get into a plane, jump into your car or make an appointment, you are risking danger, death or rejection. Risk is a daily occurrence.

Leaders know the value of risk. It's launching out into the deep while everyone else stays in the shallows. And out in the deep is where the big fish are – the ones really worth catching.

'Trust men and they will be true to you, treat them greatly and they will show themselves great.'
Ralph Waldo Emerson

Stretching Your Comfort Zone

People tend to love the familiar. The comfort zone so often has a numbing effect on our lives.

When I first started our Youth Alive events, one leader said to me, 'We've never done things like this before; the music is too loud, the speaking is too straight-forward; its all too on the edge.' And he was right. But the fruits are now evident, especially to those who have seen the impact on the thousands of lives that have been touched. While it was safe and riddled with small-minded thinking and .no-risk factors, it couldn't grow.

It's important to understand that if you're not living on the edge, *you're taking up too much space!* You see, comfort provides a sense of security. We become comfortable with all kinds of things in life – our suburb, our home, the local mall, the church we attend. With that comfort often comes complacency. It can cause us to have a lack of appreciation for what we have.

True leaders go out and launch into the area of the unknown.

Tragic Mistakes

The refusal to take risks can often lead to some tragic mistakes. A producer scored a rejection note on a manuscript that became *Gone with the Wind*. Michael Jordan once said, 'I can accept failure, everyone fails at something; but I can't accept not trying.' He should know; every time he puts on a boot he is out there taking a risk.

There is a risk to leaving our mental comfort zones. I am constantly amazed at how often people reject a business proposition or a business plan because they have a mental concept of what it is supposedly like, or have heard from a second or third hand source or a disgruntled person. Such people never venture out far enough into deep water to achieve success or attain the financial benefits they might have had. Taking the risk, taking the plunge in business is really just one of the simple risks in life.

The refusal to take risks can often lead to some tragic mistakes

Richard De Vos has said this: 'The only thing that stands between a man and what he wants from life is often merely the will to try it and the faith to believe it is possible, that is, the spirit.' A risk- taker will always have a go and believe it is possible to achieve the improbable. Have the spirit of a risk-taker!

Look for New Risks

A risk-taker is a leader who will always be looking for *a new risk*. Be the kind of person who isn't content with just one small victory; go for the bigger ones. Pele, one of the world's greatest soccer players, once said, 'The more difficult the victory, the greater the happiness in winning.'

Steve Potter has said, 'The road of success has many tempting parking-places.' We don't want to camp on our past success; we want to pursue further ones. Don't use your past victories as a hammock to sleep in but as a springboard to catapult you to greater ones! Situations and people can halt your progress temporarily, but refusing to take risks will halt you permanently.

> *The more difficult the victory, the greater the happiness in winning*

To take risks needs courage. In the words of Peter Drucker, 'Wherever you see a successful business, someone once made a courageous decision.' The courageous decision was a risk. There were probably no guarantees, only blind faith. Every time I put on an event I take a risk. There is nothing that guarantees people will come, except my belief that they will. I believe we have something they want, that only we can give them.

Taking risks may mean leaving old friends and making new ones. If you have ever moved house or moved into a new area, you will soon discover how difficult it can be to break into the existing structures that are there. It's a risk to get in, meet new friends and new acquaintances. To reach out to that new circle we need a deliberate sense of personal courage and a willingness to face possible rejection. It's risky.

The risk-taker understands there is no chance if you don't create one. We make our chances, we take our chances, we reap from our chances. Geena Davis has said, 'If you risk nothing then you risk everything.' If you're not willing to risk something, you'll never achieve anything in life.

What Risk-Taking Can Do
1. *It can create opportunities for yourself and others.*
2. *It can give you experience and knowledge.*
3. *It can create an awareness of your abilities.*
4. *It can give you a great sense of achievement.*
5. *It can expand the skill of other people.*
6. *It can break the atmosphere of doubt.*

PASSION

A further important quality for the effective relational leader is passion. Gordon MacDonald, a noted author, has said, 'The people in our world who rise to the top of business, sports, academia, science, and politics, usually do it because they are fuelled by passion.'

I am Italian – passion comes with the territory! Italians are passionate about everything. They are passionate about food and love and sport.

One needs only to go to Italy when the national soccer team is playing to notice the passion they have. I recall making the horrific blunder of trying to be served at a restaurant during one of Italy's World Cup soccer qualifiers. I discovered that you could sit there for hours but you wouldn't get served. You could threaten or even bribe, but you had very little chance, if any, of

Passion distinguishes great leaders from average leaders

getting your meal. Why? Because they love their soccer; they are passionate about it. They put themselves in the place of the players and they feel what the players feel (or at least they think they feel that way). When the team scores, the passion is electric. When the team loses, it's like walking into a funeral.

Or take Italian weddings. One of the things I love about Italian weddings is their great festivity. Apart from having an eight or nine course meal (which is right up my alley!), the singing, the dancing and the spirit of community are all completely passionate. It's a party that goes on for six or seven hours. The bride and groom go from table to table, hugging and kissing all their guests, sharing food with them, dancing in celebration of their newly- formed family. Everyone enters into a spirit of festivity flowing from this union. It is anything but boring; it is a tumultuous celebration of life, love and family.

When you leave a wedding like that you feel as though you've just fallen in love all over again with your own spouse. Why? Because of the passion you feel there – not a sensual passion but a joyful zeal and enthusiasm for the marriage that has just happened. It's contagious.

I think we Italians could really show the world how to throw a party! There is something wonderful about observing the uninhibited joy and the zest for life that passionate people have.

The Hunger that Drives You

Passion distinguishes great leaders from average leaders. Passion is that inward quality that causes you to pursue with a vengeance whatever you seek to tackle. It's that hunger to learn and to achieve which drives you.

I'm passionate about what I do; I'm passionate about the people with whom I work. I'm passionate about my dreams as a leader. Often that passion keeps me up at night, as I think creatively about issues. Sometimes I call a member of my team at odd hours, refuelling my thinking by firing ideas at them. Why? Because I'm passionate with a capital 'P'!

We should not be afraid of passion. It's a good thing to have. It keeps you lean, aggressive and open to new challenges. It keeps your blood pumping. I don't want to just shrivel up and grow old, avoiding new experiences. I want to be stretched and to stretch others. That's what keeps me young and vigorous as a leader.

Passion Overcomes Obstacles

Recently I had a very painful physical experience. I took a lunchbreak in my daily work schedule and an excruciating, almost paralysing pain came into my upper back area. I was immobilised by the intensity of the pain. I went to the doctor and he advised me to rest.

Passion will make a way where there is no way

But it was so hard to rest when I wanted to write (I was actually writing this book at the time – in fact, this chapter). The disappointment of not being able to write was worse than the pain I was feeling. Why? Because I am passionate about writing and putting thoughts on paper.

However, now I found myself temporarily incapacitated and unable to write. So, what's the next best thing? I got a dictaphone machine and talked into it. *Passion will make a way where there is no way.*

Fervour, Enthusiasm and Zeal

Passion also awakens your curiosity and keeps you going when everyone else wants you to quit. It gives you that second wind so that you can reach for the stars.

The dictionary defines passion as a 'depth of feeling toward anything that is accompanied by fervour, enthusiasm and zeal.' Passion is the wood in the fire, the fuel in the car – without it nothing seems to work. It supplies that extraordinary zest and quality of living that causes you to live above the humdrum or the ordinary. It stops you being satisfied with mundane and easy accomplishments.

Think of any great novel and you will find a passionate author. Think about a great business and you will find a passionate entrepreneur. One of the greatest needs of our youth is passion. People tell me young people are rebellious. That may be true in some cases, but I find the greatest lack or character fault in youth is their evident lack of passion.

As leaders we need to be passionate about our people and about our devotion to them. Being passionate about our vision will motivate both ourselves and our people. We need to be passionate in our service of others as well – passionate in our service of our family, our peers, our associates and our business colleagues.

Passion like this is contagious and helps to build strong relationships with others. It joins people in a common cause and purpose, and this is essential to relational leadership.

Passion – The Attitude Check

I am a real stickler for keeping the right attitude, and I find that passion is one of those things which keeps my attitude in check. It keeps me doing things with a glad heart rather than just going through the motions. According to the Marketing and Research Corporation of Princeton, New Jersey, 50-80% of Americans are in the wrong job. If you are in the wrong job, there is no way you are going to be passionate about it.

It's hard to be passionate if you are in the wrong place at the wrong time, and for all the wrong reasons. However, when you are doing something you love, you are in the *right* place; and it's always the *right* time; and you are doing it for all the *right* reasons. That's what keeps you passionate. Passion and joy are synonymous. The passion we have for everyday living is an infectious quality in a leader. It's what attracts others to our cause.

Different Passions

Everyone has different passions. Some people are really passionate about sports, others about computers, others about their garden or their pets. David Kiersey and Marilyn Bates wrote a book in 1978 entitled, *Please Understand Me*. On the second page they offered this exceptional insight, 'We have different motives, purposes, aims, values, needs, drives, impulses, urges. Nothing is more fundamental than that. We believe differently, we think, recognise, conceptualise, perceive, understand, comprehend, cogitate differently. And of course, matters of acting [and] emoting, governed as they are by wants

Whatever personality type you have, show your passion

and beliefs, follow suit and differ radically among people.'

Because of differences in our personalities, beliefs and urges, we also show our passion in different ways. For example, someone who is melancholic in personality (melancholics are generally creative people) may show their passion through their music. As for me, being a sanguine-choleric, I show passion through excitement, zeal and doing things. Whatever personality type you have, show your passion, because that passion will be the fuel for getting things done.

Passion doesn't have to be loud; it can be quiet, too. Passion is about feeling and expression more than volume. How many times have you heard a beautiful love song that is soft yet filled with great passion? Passion is usually visible, though, and it becomes the dividing wall between achievement and mediocrity. With a sense of passion you throw everything you have, your strength of mind, will, emotion and muscle, into your work with all zest and with a sense of purpose.

I recall going to a meeting once to hear an 80-year-old preacher. He didn't have the physical movements of a young speaker, but the depth of passion in his message and voice was captivating and moving. He left the younger speakers on the day for dead. What's more, we all wanted to build a relationship with this man, because his passion made him a truly relational leader.

How to Stay Passionate
As a relational leader, with all the demands of men-

torees, planning, vision, not to mention the daily demands of overseeing your enterprise, it's easy to lose your passion. This happens from time to time, so what can you do about it? Try the following:

1. Stick with what you are good at.

Be true to yourself and what you have purposed to do. Know your gifts and your strengths and let them complement your weaknesses. This will help to keep you passionate.

My gift is motivating and loving people. I make no apology for that. If you hang around me long enough, I will keep talking to you about people – people are my business and my business is people. I know my gift is in this area, so I do the best I can to keep focussed on working with people – especially the young and business leaders, my two passions in life.

I need to know what makes me tick as a person. To put it simply, it's a calling, and I need to know what my calling is, my purpose and drive, so that I can remain passionate.

2. Be willing to pay the cost.

The only way to really taste great victories is to put everything you have into winning them. It will cost you greatly to be successful but it will be worth it.

Passion fuels the fire to make the sacrifices necessary for success. Winston Churchill said, 'I have nothing to offer but blood, toil, tears, and sweat.' For many people, the term 'blood' is a turn off; sacrifice to them is a price paid by either zealous fanatics or blind fools. But there is nothing more rewarding (and it will keep your passion ignited!) than seeing the reward and celebrating the victory of service and sacrifice.

3. Be creative.
Use that entrepreneurial flair you have. How do I personally remain creative? I need time to think. I need to fill myself with good thoughts, and my body needs to be free of fatigue so that my mind can think clearly. Creative juices will then flow because of passion.

4. Have a desperate desire to succeed.
Vince Lombardi once said that winning is a habit. Unfortunately, so is losing. We must develop the passion to win. I've yet to meet the team who didn't care about winning yet actually won. Every competitive team is driven by the passion to win and not to lose or to draw.

5. Don't be threatened by other talented people.
Nothing robs you of passion and vision more than a threatened disposition. Learn to enjoy and align yourself with other people's success. Thomas Jefferson said, 'We confide in our strength, without boasting of it, we respect that of others, without fearing it.'

6. Work on your weaknesses.
Don't be discouraged but use them as a springboard to personal development so you can excel.

7. Identify what you are passionate about.

Ask yourself, 'What do I think about more than anything else? What is the thing that drives me?' Next, ask yourself what you would do with your life if you knew you couldn't fail. What excites you and will keep you passionate? This passion will cause you to stretch further, to leave your comfort zone and to tackle that impossible task.

CONVICTION

Conviction is absolutely essential to the effective relational leader. You have to have gut-feelings, principles and a sense of integrity, and you must have the courage to act on them.

Ken Blanchard and Don Shula have written a great book entitled *Everyone's a Coach*. In it they discuss being 'conviction-driven.' Being conviction-driven means doing the right thing for the right reasons.

Effective leaders must have boundaries and reference points. Convictions will be their compass to determine what they seek in life, how they operate and how they

> *Effective leaders must have boundaries and reference points*

maintain a solid course. Beliefs and convictions are also important because they determine the boundaries within which people can work with you. They spell out the length and breadth of relationship with you.

I think it was John Cougar Mellencamp who said, 'If you won't stand for something you will fall for anything.' In *Dreamers Never Sleep* I mentioned the difference between living by conviction and living by preference. People couldn't care less about their *preferences*, but they will die for their *convictions*. A lack of conviction is like a river without banks – just one huge, muddy puddle.

That's why it's important to understand the power of convictions. Having convictions gives us momentum and a sense of direction. Unfortunately, sometimes individuals and organisations can lack convictions, and therefore they lack the direction and the momentum to keep going.

Core Beliefs

Leaders must always ask themselves what their core beliefs are. What is the heartbeat of your organisation? It's your beliefs and convictions which cause you to action things and make them happen, and it's beliefs that ultimately come true.

Beliefs come out of your dreams, and dreams keep you motivated to fulfil your beliefs. To a leader, convictions and beliefs become the filter, the catalyst and the coal for the fire in an organisation.

In our organisation, a core conviction is that we can make a difference to other people, particularly to the young and to business people. We believe we can motivate others to a life of excellence. We believe we can lift their standard of performance from 'just working' to being a significant contributor. We believe young people do not have to be drug-dependent, lonely, depressed, or carry an attitude, but can be part of the solution rather than the problem. It's all just a part of our core belief.

Sticking to Convictions

It's the convictions of an organisation and a leader that give him or her a sense of pride, and also give followers a sense of pride and direction. Good leaders hold to their convictions.

I have convictions I hold to very dearly. They are near to my faith and values as a person. I often read books and articles presenting opposite views to my beliefs. Why? Because I want to strengthen what I do believe. I don't fear what others say; I have my own mind. But some people never venture to read something out of their comfortable box, and that is a sign of weakness.

Convictions are not negotiable and are not for sale

A few years ago a business friend invited me out to lunch to introduce me to some influential people. They had heard about our work with youth and wanted to be financial contributors. That was music to my ears. When you work with young people you need all the financial help you can get, especially from the corporate sector. After brief introductions we sat down to eat.

The influential lady started to ask me some questions about my vision and our direction which I was only too happy to unload. She was impressed, to say the least, but then came the clincher. She asked questions relating to my faith. In the end she said, 'Mr Mesiti, my colleagues and I would be happy to contribute $100,000 to your organisation (of course, tax deductible!). However, we would like you to drop the faith factor, the God bit.' I was numb.

Now understand, at this point we were in desperate financial need, up to our eyeballs in debt and with no visible means of getting out of it. I was suddenly faced with a choice: what's negotiable and what isn't? I kindly thanked them for the lunch, then said this: 'There *are* some negotiable factors in life, but God isn't one of them. I've come this far with God and any success I have is because of faith. I leave here without your money but with my faith.'

What happened next couldn't have been more timely. As we left the lunch and walked into the street, a burly guy came running after me out of a nearby computer shop. He said, 'Pat, when I was a kid I was on drugs – suicidal and depressed. I came to one of your meetings and found my faith. That decision changed my life. Now I own this computer shop, I have a beautiful wife and a great family.' We hugged and rejoiced. I turned around to my startled, influential friends and said, 'One hundred grand can't buy that!'

Convictions must be repeated over and over again. Just as in primary school you studied your multiplication-tables over and over again, in different ways and in different settings, so it is with convictions.

You can't truly lead or mentor others without a strong

internal rule that keeps you moving toward your core objectives. And these objectives must be values-based

DESIRE

The next quality of a relational leader is desire. The Collins dictionary defines 'desire' this way: 'to yearn for the possession of, to request, to entreat; a longing.' I like that: 'to yearn for, to entreat, to long for'. Every one of those words is potent. Every leader who is going to lead people and relate to people, needs to have a desire, a longing, a yearning.

The desire to serve, the desire to excel, the desire to achieve, the desire to empower, the desire to impact – these are the key ingredients. A leader without desire is like a car without petrol. The mechanical condition may be right, but if there is no fuel the car

It's desire that causes you to stop being a spectator and to become a player on the field

will never run. Desire is like a fuel that gets put into an engine and causes it to ignite and take off. It's desire that causes you to stop being a spectator and to become a player on the field. It's desire that helps you do your best and to give your best.

Enjoyment – A Key to Desire
One of the keys to desire is enjoyment. I find it hard not

to enjoy the things I desire. As a leader you will note that the things you desire are the things you enjoy.

Here's a tip. If you don't enjoy something, more than likely it's not a real desire. I enjoy people; my desire is to see them grow. I enjoy reading; my desire is to read more and accumulate more knowledge. I enjoy not only reaching a goal but the journey toward the goal, too.

In his book *On Becoming a Leader*, Warren Bennis says, 'Only when we know what we are made of and what we want to make of it can we begin our lives, and we must do it despite an unwitting conspiracy of people and events against us.' 'When we know what we are made of and what we want to make of it' must refer to desire, pure and simple. Do you desire to hold power, or to enable people by giving it away? As a leader your desire should be to release people.

> *'Leaders enable others to act not by hoarding the power they have but by giving it away.'*
>
> **Kouzes Posner**

One desire of a leader should always be to act as a model for the organisation to follow. Behaviour causes people to respect and honour you as a leader, and that's something a leader must desire.

The desire to innovate, take risks, experiment, be creative, or find a better way of doing things – to be an originator – is another desire crucial to leadership.

The Desire to Inspire

A leader can never command respect or commitment; they can *only* inspire it. Inspiration comes through giving vision, direction and significance. Enthusiasm, zeal and commitment are contagious; they spread from leader to followers. Effective leaders desire to inspire.

One of the great keys to inspiring people is not dwelling on the past but on the future. You can learn from the past but it won't inspire you. It's your future that ignites inspiration. Relational leaders (who must be inspirational leaders) will prefer to talk about the future rather than the past.

They will also inspire people through cooperation and collaboration, building spirit in the team and in the organisation. This happens when they give people a sense of capability and empowerment. Making people feel they are powerful, strong and important in their own right leads to success. Inspiration taps into people's hearts and minds; a leader inspires people to act from the heart not just from the head.

> *A leader can never command respect or commitment, they can only inspire it*

BOUNCING BACK

Leaders need to be like rubber balls and just keep bouncing back! The ability to strike back from adversity, regroup, reorganise and get going again, rather than lamenting and stewing over past mistakes, failures, disappointments or hurts, is one of the greatest attributes of a leader. People can easily crumble when they fail, make a mistake or wrongly assess something, but the strength of a leader is truly determined in the ability to bounce back.

Martina Navratilova lost twenty-one of her first twenty-four matches against her arch-rival Chris Evert. She resolved to hit more freely on the big points, and in the ensuing transformation beat Evert thirty-nine out of their next fifty-seven matches. No woman tennis player has ever won as many matches or tournaments. The first children's book written by Theodore S. Geisel (you know him as Dr Seuss) was rejected by twenty-three publishers. The twenty-fourth publisher sold six million copies. Both Martina Navratilova and Theodore Geisel mastered the art of bouncing back.

The art of turning tragedy into investment is one a leader must re-develop over and over again

The art of turning tragedy into investment is one a leader must re-develop over and over again. For as long as you are involved in leadership, you will have failures and flops. Leaders require the inner emotional and spiritual resolve to bounce back from the life-jolting tragedies which so easily cripple others. It's not that we pursue misfortune, disadvantage, problems or failures; they come our way regardless. It's the leaders' leader who is able to pull together inner resources and launch out again, setting his or her sails to catch what's left of the gale.

To learn from past failures and mistakes is to not be crippled by them. A very wise man once said that the only difference between stumbling blocks and stepping stones is the way we use them.

The relational leader is a big-thinker characterised by passion, desire, the will to win and a *jois de vive*, no matter how tough times get. Such a person is conviction-driven, relying upon deeply-held inner values to sustain and nourish their dreams, so that they keep growing, building and nurturing relationships with the big people they retain all around them. By so doing, they accomplish deeds greater than others can ever imagine. They are risk-takers who take a chance on dreams and put their faith in the hands of those who assist them. Such people are truly effective relational leaders who go on to build big people.

> *The only difference between stumbling blocks and stepping stones is the way we use them*

CHAPTER FOUR

THE LEADER AND FAMILY LIFE

It is often said that charity begins at home. I believe leadership also begins at home. I heard a speaker once take a biblical phrase and change it in the context of family; he asked, 'What does it profit a man if he gains the whole world and loses his own children?' The implications of this statement have stayed with me ever since.

You see, our children are not just a commodity or an appendage. They are both our future and our present.

Mario Cuomo has said, 'Leaders need to develop the lives of their children as much, if not more so, than the lives of the people in their corporation, their associates, and their peers.' The same principles that govern our leadership in the lives of others are the principles to apply in the lives of our children.

To be a successful leader is to be successful at home. I often cringe at the way the Western world treats children. Think for a moment on how we treat them – how we use them, abuse them, ignore them, discard them, reject them, trade them and sacrifice them on the altar of career. Is it any wonder we have run-away children?

Children Need to Grow

Children need to grow, and *Proverbs*, the Bible's ancient collection of wisdom, teaches us we need to 'train them up in the way they should go.' Training is not just teaching and verbalising. It is overseeing, demonstrating and allowing them to practise what they learn. If it was just left to verbal communication, raising our children would be simple. You could merely program them via your words and they would act out what you say. But like everyone else, children need

To be a successful leader is to be successful at home

not only verbal input but monitoring, encouragement, strengthening and nurturing. This training starts as early as the crib and goes right through to their teen and adolescent years.

As good coaches bring out the best in respective team members, so parent-leaders bring out the best in their respective children. Parents instil values in their children. While I could write volumes on the subject, what I want to do is give you a brief synopsis to help you as a leader – whether in business, church, community or professional life – to lead your children and bring out the best in their lives.

Children, just like the business or organisation you are involved with and the people you are leading, need development. They require strategies, vision, direction and help to find the best in themselves. But unlike a business, kids *feel* – they are able to cry and laugh because they have souls and emotions.

Being a Kid Today

What's it like being a kid today? It's certainly different from when you and I were children.

Dr E.V. Hill, the great preacher, once said, 'Today's youth is a special kind. This kind has never known a newspaper without a war headline; this kind has had all the opportunity to see on television open pornography and smut unknown to any age.'

The Internet, CD ROM technology and the like have changed the world forever. Today, a child can interact via a computer with thousands of people all over the world, yet many of them cannot hold a simple human conversation beyond the level of 'yes', 'no' or 'because.' They can travel the world and communicate on computers, but they can't seem to talk face-to-face with people.

Our young are lacking a moral compass as never before

We need to realise our teenagers represent the most entertained, high-tech, fast-paced culture that has ever existed. But we also need to realise they are the most relationless, drug-dependent, suicidal and depressed generation of all time

A Different Generation

Here are some things which make young people today different from any previous generation.

1. *They are desperate for authenticity.* They want to know what it's like to be real, to feel, to struggle and to overcome. They are not interested in glossing over issues and problems. They feel more than any other generation.

2. *They are hungry for community.* Many people have stated that the theme of this generation is not 'how to get ahead' but 'how to get along'. Just look around you and see the way they rally behind the causes. Why is that? Because they have a sense of community and a lack of dogmatism.

3. *They lack a mora. compass.* To our young there is no exclusive right or wrong lifestyle. But neither do they have an 'if it feels good, do it' mentality. It's more like, 'If I say it's right, it's right; if I say it's wrong, it's wrong.' Our young are lacking a moral compass as never before.

4. *They are angry.* There is an unprecedented anger in this generation. From singer Tori Amos to Alannis Morisett and Radio-Head, you can hear the anger and pain, not only in their lyrics but in the way they sing. Songs like 'Pure Massacre' and

'Creep' show the anguish and concern they have for marital and family breakdown, as well as for their own inadequate self images. Songs that declare 'I'm a creep' do not promote a good, positive self image in a child.

5. *They focus on the arts.* Today's young people don't want to be bored. They have grown up in a high-tech, multi-image environment, so they are focussed on artistic and creative development. Where previous generations geared themselves more to career, business and kids, today's youth are geared more toward fashion, communication, music, dance and performance. If you look at some of the most powerful productions today you will see they are stage-shows that incorporate the crowd.

6. *They are hurting.* The anger of this generation stems from hurt. They feel hurt about being ripped off with respect to the future. They face job insecurity and increased debt. The previous generation got into so much debt, neither they nor their children will be able to pay it all back. This has only contributed to further alienation, hurt and a consequent increase in the generation gap.

They are a generation struggling to believe there is a future. That's why it's imperative for parents to instil in them a hope for the future.

7. *They have a visible lack of spontaneity.* In simple terms, in a high-tech society the worst sin of both computers and humans is to be unpredictable. A techno-society runs more smoothly when everyone

cooperates and does the predictable thing, on time and without fuss.

As a consequence, our youth have been robbed of individuality. A high-tech society is not ultimately interested in what is unique to each individual, but what is identical, quantifiable and measurable. The techno-society wants what can be counted, standardised and computerised so that our young people are robbed of their individuality.

8. *They have been robbed of self-consciousness.* The more you can reduce a person's awareness, the more you can get him or her away from thinking, and it's easy to control people when they are not thinking. We must encourage our young to be thinkers – indeed, free-thinkers.

HOW TO LOVE YOUR KIDS

If these are the challenges facing today's young people, what are some of the answers? What do parent-leaders need to do to support, love, nurture and effectively 'train' their children?

Parent-leaders need to respond to their kids in love and with a deep sense of wanting to make their world better.

Be Authentic at Home

I believe leaders must be authentic people in their family lives, And that means being real.

Parents, your kids expect you to be Mum and Dad.

They don't expect you to be Madonna or Michael Jackson. Coming home in a mini-skirt, fish-net stockings and high heels with your midriff poking out is not conducive to a 'Mum' image!

Kids hate a lack of authenticity. Be authentic; be yourself; and for goodness' sake, *be real!*

Help your children understand that life is not a destination but a journey

As a relational leader you must be a leader in your home, too. So show the struggles you face and the journey you travel to overcome them. Help your children understand that life is not a destination but a journey, full of mountains to climb and valleys to overcome.

Give Your Kids a Sense of Community

Significance is important not just for your employees but for your kids, too. They need a sense of purpose in belonging to a community. The same things you do to develop leaders in your organisation must be done at home to help your kids. Every child has purpose, talent, giftedness, individuality and a very genuine uniqueness. Focus on these things and build their sense of importance.

It's also important to tell them *why* they are significant by highlighting their achievements and not holding their failures over their heads like a bomb. Significance is the most important aspect in a child's growth and development because it produces a sense of ability, confidence and self-worth. Just like adults (and please remember, adults are just children in bigger bodies), kids have a spirit and a soul which never grows old and is the same size when they reach adulthood as the day they were born.

Encourage Excellence

Help your children to understand that perfection is never the goal in life – excellence is. When kids strive to be perfect – or when parents pressure them to strive for perfection – it can send them into a tailspin of despair.

Help your children understand that perfection is never the goal in life - excellence is

In such circumstances people fear more failure and often become despondent and give up trying. Perfectionists can be vulnerable to every kind of mood swing and emotional projection, so failure becomes a threat and totally unacceptable to them.

A parent-leader must never fall into 'performance trap' thinking which says your household has to be a 'Brady Bunch.' No kid has to *measure up*, they just need help to *grow up*.

Let Your Kids Take Risks

A parent-leader allows kids to take risks. When you strive for perfection in children, there is an inevitable fear of failure which, as a consequence, leads you to reduce the element of risk. Allow your kids to take some risks.

My parents would not allow me to go swimming for fear I would drown. (That's a recipe for raising a maladjusted Italian communicator – but I digress.) Their fear created a fear of water in me. It also created an inability to swim which to this day still haunts me. (Fortunately, I have followers who can swim for me!). But there is hope: I have a new pair of floaties and I'm doing quite well.

Give Your Kids a Moral Compass

Kids need a moral compass just as adults do. As a parent-leader your job is to provide it. This is not bashing them over the head with values like thunder-claps; it's just helping them to find values-based bearings.

We all need to find 'true north' in our values. Steer them in the right direction in such a way that your boundaries do not restrict, but rather launch them. Discipline is not an enemy; it is a true friend.

Today, more than ever before, our young want to do what's right. A kid said this to me once at a public high school: 'Why doesn't somebody show me how to live? Why are people scared to tell me what's right and wrong? How can I make up my own mind when I've never been given any boundaries?' Young people are craving boundaries, and they need them.

As a leader in the work force you are comfortable setting boundaries, and you should be equally comfortable setting boundaries at home. Behaviour is the reflection of core beliefs – beliefs about who we are and what we believe to be right and wrong. Therefore, it is important to give kids a compass to live by. In the movie *Mr Holland's Opus*, the high school principal challenges Mr Holland by telling him that, as a teacher, he is a compass. I am here to tell you, so are parents.

Accept Your Children

Adults relate to their leaders on the basis of acceptance. When they feel trusted, accepted and valued, then they perform at amazing levels. If leaders can make people feel accepted, loved and worthwhile, they will flourish.

It's the same with kids. When kids are given a sense of worth and find out that acceptance is given, not based on performance, they tend to rise to new heights.

There is a big difference, however, between acceptance and attention. Most people crave acceptance but often only get the cheap substitute, attention. For example, many teenagers find that taking drugs gains them entry into a particular peer group made up of others who take drugs. They take this as *acceptance*, but it is really only momentary attention.

> *Most people crave acceptance but often only get the cheap substitute, attention*

Parent-leaders must give young people a sense of acceptance, not based on performance or winning but *just because they are themselves*. A child's search for significance demands that he or she be accepted not on performance but as a valuable and loved human being.

Many people say 'I love my kids,' and I would agree they probably do. But do they accept them *regardless* of their educational, sporting or other achievements? Do they accept them for just being themselves?

Let me give you a few words of advice on what you should never do to your kids:

- Don't compare them with your other children.
- Don't compare them with *other people's* children.
- Get to the bottom of their struggles rather than just deal with symptoms.
- Don't try and redeem your own failures in life through them (for example, don't do the old 'I could have risen to the top in life, but because I did not, you will' number).

Don't force your children into being what you think you should or could have been. Just let them be and build acceptance and confidence in their own skills and abilities. Tell them they are loved, show them they are loved, and prove to them they are loved – especially when they make mistakes.

Support Your Kids in Mistakes

Foolishness is bound up in the heart of a child. Children do foolish things and it's up to the parent-leader to steer them through their mistakes and to help them build a strong foundation in life.

Children, just like adults, thrive on praise. There are two times to praise your kids – when they're doing great and when they're failing, when they deserve it and when they don't. Above all, *allow for failures*. Don't go off the deep end. Don't panic. And don't go to a shrink!

Failures will happen. They are normal. Just keep communicating with your kids.

Give Your Kids Heroes

Children need heroes. I want to be a hero to my kids, but I also want to surround them with people to admire. Many children have heroes. Unfortunately, some of them are not true heroes.

Surround your children with people who are worthwhile following – high-achievers and great leaders. Every time we have a guest, a music group, a well-known speaker or a celebrity at our events, I watch my children develop a sense of significance and importance in meeting these heroes. It doesn't have to be U2, either. Every kid looks up to someone. It's up to you to find out who it is.

Our kids are neither pegs nor holes, neither round nor square

I will never forget the day a famous singing group came for dinner at our home. We flew them to Australia for one of our major festivals, and the kids in the youth group were envious when they came to our house to eat. It was wonderful watching my kids respond and to see their sense of pride and self-worth as they showed the photos of this group to others.

You might not know high profile celebrities, and that's okay. Make celebrities out of the people you do know. Find out who your kids admire and be sure you allow them sufficient time with these people. My own children have some fantastic role models to follow. Seeing my two girls grow up with a desire to mimic worthwhile heroes is a great joy.

Release Your Children in their Gifts

Each child is unique. Our two daughters are so different from each other it's frightening. One, Rebecca, is creative, a performer, a party person (in a good sense!). The other, Chantelle, is a reader, a thinker and a feeler. Rebecca wants to be a singer; Chantelle has probably changed vocational goals twenty-five times since I started writing this book. However, they are both very, very special.

Parent leaders have the responsibility to strengthen their children's gifts and complement their weaknesses

Sometimes parents try to fit square pegs into round holes. Our kids are neither pegs nor holes, neither round nor square. Don't try to force them into a particular mould. It's important to train them up in the way they should go.

Parent-leaders have the responsibility to strengthen their children's gifts and complement their weaknesses.

Rebecca is not a great reader, so to motivate her in that area we pay her for reading books. She doesn't need to be encouraged to sing and practise piano; she loves that. Chantelle, however, loves to read, so we pay her to practise piano. Why pay them? It's an incentive program. Adults love incentives and so do kids. Give them incentives where they are weak and encourage them in their gifts.

Share the Action

Let your children in on the action. It's important that parents involve children in their lives in every way. This may mean, for example, taking them on a trip to the office. Many parents spend too much time at work, and sometimes, even when they are at home, they are still at work and forget to let their kids look into the window of their world.

It's extremely important to tell your children what's going on in the 'grown-ups' world – in your business, your friendships, your meetings, your travels. You must make them feel a part of what you're doing.

Children should never be the victims of our leadership. They should learn from it and grow. This will always mean allowing them to be a part of your world.

MIND YOUR LANGUAGE

When I was discussing how to treat your children's mistakes and failures, I said, 'Just keep communicating.' But there are ways and ways to communicate.

Here's how not to do it. This is a list of the seven dumbest things parents ever say:

1. *'When I was your age ...'* The fact is, this generation is so different that you have never been their age. You probably had Doris Day, but these kids have Madonna, Marilyn Manson and every other weird person you can think of. So remember, you never were their age.

2. *'Do you realise how tough it was for me to have a Coke or a hamburger when I was a kid?'* Face it, parents, they don't realise. Your kids simply don't understand when you tell them you had to climb Mount Everest just to get a can of Coke or that only the privileged few could go to McDonald's. They don't get it, so quit reminding them of it.

3. *'How was school today?'* Many parents try this as a conversation starter. Here is the incredibly awesome and deep response you will get from your kid when you ask 'How was school today?' Are you ready for it? Here it is: 'Good.'
Don't ask dumb questions like that. Ask questions requiring a greater than one word response. Otherwise, that's all you'll get. They don't teach communication at school any longer.

4. *'Do you want me to belt you?'* Parents, think about it! What do you expect your kids to say? 'Please do it slowly, Dad, I love pain'? 'Oh, Mum, I missed out last week, so can I please have two'? Questions like that invite the inevitable.

5. *'What are you doing?'* You must realise by now

your kids are always doing 'Nothin'.' One of my personal favourites is 'Where are you going?' It's always 'Nowhere.'

6. *'What do you think?'* They don't think, they feel. Ask them how they feel, because today's generation is a generation of feelers.

TRAVELLING

Many parents, and I am one of them, spend a lot of time travelling in their professional lives. This takes them away from home a lot. Here's a tip or two for parent-leaders who travel away from home regularly.

1. *Phone home, E.T.* Ensure that you call home often. I make it my aim to call home at least once every day, regardless of what it costs. Sometimes it's repetitive, but it's just wonderful to hear my kids' voices every day and to let them know I'm thinking about them. Just a few words telling them how much I love them and miss them can make all the difference.

2. *Bring back gifts for your children.* Show them that your business, your lifestyle, your travelling is not an enemy. It's not robbing them. It's giving them something back. Show the rewards of what you're doing.

3. *When at home, be at home.* Switch on and don't get too tired or too stressed. Make sure you don't give your kids the leftovers. Give them quality time.

4. *Talk about where you've been, whom you've met, what you've done.* It's amazing how hungry kids are for information. Let them in on your trip. Give them detail.

5. *Avoid being the bad guy/girl.* For example, don't keep saying to your kids, 'Wait 'til I get home!' If discipline is necessary when you get home, at least be home for some time before the discipline is given. Don't do it immediately on your arrival. The first thing to show them is love: 'I missed you' and 'I'm so happy to see you.' And remember, discipline is not punishment; it's instruction. Keep your cool and be patient.

7. *Take them along on business trips.* On a few occasions I have taken my daughters individually on trips. I once took Rebecca to New Zealand where she met some friends to whom she writes even today. Another time I took Chantelle on a trip interstate. She met a friend whom she talks about often.

8. *Never be too busy for your family.* While you're away, make sure you take their calls and, if need be, let them interrupt your schedule.

If you're on a trip and your children are in desperate need, go home immediately. A friend told me of a time when one of his children was very ill while he was on the most important business trip of his career. He graciously told his host that his family was in a crisis, his child was sick, and he had to go home. This is called setting priorities.

FUN

The last thing I want to say to the parent-leader is to be fun. Avoid being a bore. Make a lot of noise, rough-house and do whatever it takes for your kids to get the most out of you!

Bring joy, gladness, fun and laughter into your home. 'A merry heart is like a medicine,' and there are a lot of sick hearts out there. Make sure your home is a happy and joyous one.

If you do, I promise you will launch yourself out as an effective relational-leader from a secure base of operations. You can't conquer the world while your own kingdom is in revolt.

CHAPTER FIVE

LEADERSHIP AND CREDIBILITY

Today, more than ever before, people are being angered by broken promises and any hint of a lack of credibility. People are looking for credibility from government officials and those seated in the boardrooms of our vast land. The question is, *do they ever find it?*

There is a profound pain amongst our young people as they face the bleak and uncertain future of unemployment. They have no idea if there will be a future for them. What they want is credible, compassionate leadership. What they often get is a very poor substitute.

All around us, political leaders are committed verbally to world peace yet continue to build bombs to destroy entire civilisations. They promise prospects for good jobs and a furthering of education, yet education is cut dramatically in government budgets year after year. People receive promises on health, yet these same promises are cynically broken as soon as they

There is a wearying lack of integrity in words these days. Promises appear to be made only to be broken

are made. There is a wearying lack of integrity in words these days. Promises appear to be made only to be broken.

Failure of Credibility

Credibility is very high on the agenda of followers. Most of them find it very hard to distinguish between a lie and a broken promise. Let me illustrate.

Dad comes home and makes a promise to his son to go fishing on Friday. All week, the son dreams about going fishing with his father and the great time they will have. He gets his fishing rod ready – he's excited. He tells his friends at school.

Friday morning comes; he's anxious and excited. Unfortunately, Dad has just 'remembered' he has a football game to go to with his friends. Dad explains to his son that something has come up, there is a

Wrong perceptions based on wrong assumptions lead to wrong conclusions, for all the right reasons

game he forgot about and he has to go out. Suddenly, the dream has been shattered.

How does a child determine whether Dad is lying or just broke a promise? It's a little hard to distinguish between the two, don't you think? That's how people feel when leaders fail to keep their word.

One of life's tragedies goes like this: *Wrong* perceptions based on *wrong* assumptions lead to *wrong* conclusions, for all the *right* reasons. The wrong perception can be as simple as 'Dad probably never intended to take me.' This leads to a wrong assumption: 'Dad really cares more about football than about me.' Of course, the wrong conclusion is an inevitable consequence: 'I'm not important.'

Credibility in leadership helps others gain the right perception and reach the right conclusions. If credibility is damaged it must immediately be restored. For leaders this means, for example, that if a promise can't be kept, deal with it immediately, and be sure to explain your position. Don't ever excuse your failures.

Character

A credible leader will always achieve more and do more than a merely charismatic leader. Charisma is vitally important – you have to make others believe in your cause. But character is essential. Charisma grows very stale in the confined space of a glass-house. Followers see you every minute of the day. To maintain this successfully, leaders must cultivate the right attitudes toward everything they do.

Effective relational leaders need not only a positive attitude but also a generous spirit – the kind of spirit which releases people into excellence. They need an untiring attitude when people try to cramp their space and take their time. They need an attitude of service, an attitude of winning, an attitude of courtesy, an attitude of faith and an attitude of kindness and forgiveness.

A credible leader will always achieve and do more than a merely charismatic leader

Credible leaders never look out only for number one. Great leaders grow big people by looking out for numbers two, three and four. They learn to make others number one.

Establishing and maintaining credibility is one of the most important things a relational leader ever does. There are many factors involved in credibility, but in this chapter I will focus on three areas of vital concern:

- Trust and accessibility.
- Being true to your core values.
- Consistency in attitude and ethical life.

TRUST AND ACCESSIBILITY

The basis of credibility in the leader-follower relationship is trust. Leaders need to grow in trust.

People tend to trust those they know. The invisible bogiemen, usually referred to as 'they', are *out there* and *mistrusted*, no matter who 'they' may be. 'They' may be government, corporate officials or some similar nameless, faceless, powerful hierarchy. As a relational leader you must not fall into this category.

Let me ask you a simple question: Is it easier to trust someone who builds a close relationship with you, or to mistrust them? What about someone you only hear about at a distance? The answer is obvious.

Leaders who want to build trust and credibility must get close to people. They must cultivate the skill of shaking hands. They must enhance their visibility through the person-to-person approach.

Accessibility Produces Trust

In my travels, I am often asked to speak to business groups, particularly by my friends in the Interactive Distribution business. Most of their leaders lead busy lives. They are financially independant but terribly busy, yet their accessibility never ceases to amaze me.

The basis of credibility in the leader-follower relationship is trust

They can travel from a function costing hundreds. of thousands of dollars, and the very next night stay in a living-room somewhere, sleeping on torn-up carpet in a broken down apartment. They make themselves accessible to the real people; they are highly visible; they are people of good reputation and they are to be trusted.

The loyalty shown to the these leaders is amazing. Every leader should learn this lesson in relational leadership. They shake hands, talk and communicate, even if they don't know everybody personally or by name. They remain visible and touchable. There is a sense of 'Hey, they're one of us!'

Accessibility produces trust. One of King Solomon's proverbs says, 'He who isolates himself rises against all wise judgment.' Every leader who isolates him or herself from the crowd rages against all wisdom. Leaders who isolate themselves cut off both their own potential and the future of their followers.

The vine gives life to the branches. If you cut down the vine everything withers and dies. Building trust means growing a 'we' and 'us' mentality.

BEING TRUE

It is not always easy to maintain trust, however. After all, there are good days and bad days, rough sailing and smooth. How does one maintain trust, reputation and credibility in the bad times as well as the good?

Maintaining credibility in difficult times requires clear thinking. Sometimes it's easy to compromise on a seemingly insignificant principle, especially when it makes for an easier road or when compromise proves a more profitable alternative.

The first thing to remember in maintaining credibility is that it is never easy. It takes strength, persistence, discipline and character. In fact, there are six key elements to credibility. I will list them here, and then we can examine them one by one:

- Be true to yourself.

- Be true to your followers.
- Be true to you values.
- Be true to your long-term dreams.
- Be true to you purpose and your vision.
- Be true to your principles and beliefs.

Be True to Yourself

One of the basic tenets of Greek religion was inscribed on their temples: Know thyself. Dan Caplan, president of Hertz car rental corporation, has said, 'I know who I was, who I am and where I want to be.' Every leader must have this same sense of steadfast conviction. The better you know yourself, the better you will understand situations of conflict.

Leaders seeking to maintain credibility must be true to themselves. Your principles and core values must come first. Profit, exploitation and deception are never core values in leadership. Don't lead out of fear that you might get caught, but out of respect for the truth. Moral choices, not fear of being caught, should motivate us to maintain our credibility and reputation.

The better you know yourself the better the decisions you will make

Leaders in the 1990s need greater ability to decipher the often conflicting and ambiguous messages all around. The better you know yourself, the better the decisions you will make. Your clear mind will help you unravel difficult situations.

There is a wonderful story about King Solomon in
the Bible. A dispute arose between two women. Both
had given birth to baby boys. Unfortunately, one of the
women lost her son at birth. They both claimed to be
the mother of the living child. Solomon was asked to
make a decision. He said he
would cut the boy in half and
give half to each mother. *Strong leadership is*
One mother cried out, 'No, I *built on mutual*
would rather the other *understanding and*
woman had him.' Solomon *respect*
gave the son to this mother.
He had no intention of cut-
ting the boy in half, but he knew in himself the principle
that mothers always protect. He was true to what he
believed, and his gut instinct showed him the correct
course.

Leaders must ask constantly: Who am I? What do I
believe? What do I stand for? What are my convictions?
You must clarify your own convictions, beliefs and values. Once they are clear you can incorporate them and
translate them into guiding lights both for yourself and
your organisation.

I have tried to instil my own values in my organisation. We have guiding principles to govern our events:
they must be excellent (excellence is one of our core
commitments); they must have character and be above
reproach; and they must be contemporary and relevant
to young people. We then find young men and women
gifted in dance, drama, music and technical areas to

implement the vision. But everything flows from our core values. This helps us to maintain our credibility.

Be True to Your Followers

Leaders must be true to their followers. We are not here to lead them up the garden path. Strong leadership is built on mutual respect and understanding.

Followers come to believe in their leaders and to see them as worthy of their trust when they believe their leaders have their best interests at heart. Therefore, you cannot only be seen to be true to your followers; you must actually *be* true to your followers. Reach out to them, care for them, listen to them, talk to them, ask them questions, be compassionate to them. Help them fulfil their desires and dreams.

Be True to Your Values

Credibility entails being true to your values. As we saw in an earlier chapter, all organisations must have common, core values to bind them together. An organisation with conflicting values will never survive. Shared values become the glue which binds an organisation together. In difficult times, always return to your core values and stick to them.

Be True to Your Long-term Dream

Credibility is built when we are true to our long-term dream. It's important to have a long-term dream. Every dream is a journey, never a destination.

You will have some ups and downs, but it's important

to remain true to your dream, even in the down times. Never give up and never quit.

When difficult times come, understand that adversity gives birth to greatness. Out of tragedy triumph is born.

Credibility is built when we are true to our long-term dream ... every dream is a journey not a destination

The greatest day in any life is the day of birth. With every birth, a new purpose enters the world. Hang on to those long-term dreams and be true to your purpose.

Be True to Your Purpose and Vision

When followers watch you closely and observe that you have remained faithful to your purpose, credibility is born. People long to see a consistent life-long pattern in their leaders. It gives them a rich sense of security, knowing leaders won't change from one day to the next or with every new breeze that blows through town.

Keep your purpose clear, simple and honourable, and be faithful to it. Others will believe in it when you do.

Be True to Your Principles and Beliefs

Having principles is integral to all leadership. Beliefs and principles are what drive us. Always be true to your principles. Don't waffle or take a backward step as a leader. Be clear and precise about principles. The world is full of ambiguity and greyness; make a difference by standing out from the crowd.

ATTITUDE

Attitude and Altitude

Leaders must grow in attitude. A wise man has said, your attitude determines your altitude. The attitudes we carry towards people, towards ourselves, towards our vision, towards our mistakes – these will determine the altitude of our development and growth.

Fear of failure, for example, is an attitude to be concerned about. Albert Hubbard once said, 'The greatest mistake you can make in life is continually fearing you will make one.' Great leaders have an attitude of rising above the crowd when it seems to want to shout them down. James Cook said, 'The man who wants to lead the orchestra must turn his back on the crowd.' An attitude of persistence, when everything else tells you to slow down, stop and give up, is a winning attitude.

Your attitude determines your altitude

In his book *Man's Search for Meaning*, Viktor Frankl says this: 'We have a right to choose our attitude.' Frankl was speaking about his painful and trying experience of life in a German concentration camp. He was taken away and stripped of his family, his dignity, his clothes and his future. He was made to dig for food with his bare hands in the frozen ground. But his tormentors could not take away his right to choose his attitude – and because of this he was a free man, freer even than his guards. His conclusion: 'Ultimate freedom is a man's right to choose his attitude.'

Attitudes Under Control

On a recent trip to the USA I had to fly from New Mexico to Dallas, Texas. A mere sixty minute flight turned into a chaotic sixteen hour nightmare.

When we took off, the plane could not reach the correct altitude because of mechanical difficulties, so we had to turn back for repairs. Two hours later we took off again. Once more we encountered engine problems. The captain said that in twenty years of flying he had never had such a terrible experience. We lined up to reschedule our flights. But a really bad day was about to get even worse. Dallas was hit with severe storms – no

'Ultimate freedom is a man's right to choose his attitude'

Viktor Frankl

flights into Dallas. Terrific! You can imagine the chaos at the airport.

If you're anything like me, you hate waiting in lines. Looking at the length of the lines, I knew I was in for the mother of all delays. I could feel my attitude starting a negative dive on the temper altimeter. Tempers were flaring all around me.

So, I made a decision to keep my cool and bite my tongue. After all, what could I do about the weather? It took three hours of queuing to get to the counter. The options were to wait for the next flight, six hours away, or fly to Denver, then Dallas. I chose this option. Typical 'A' type that I am, I thought, 'At least I'll be moving.'

I had to keep checking my attitude until I finally got to Dallas.

Why Me?

Just recently we put on a three-day outdoor event for teenagers. We had planned it for two years. Friday night was a beautiful evening until a few light showers started to fall. Saturday was far worse; it didn't bother to rain, it just poured. Sunday poured, too.

During the weekend I was commuting from our event to another function. On my return from the airport it was pouring with rain. I looked up and said, 'Why me? What did I do wrong?' My attitude bubbled up into anger and caused a knot in my stomach.

There are some things a bad attitude can't change, but a good attitude will see you through

I realised I had to take a quick stock-take. I'd done all I could. I'd prayed, cried, worried and stressed. None of it was going to change the weather. The only thing which could change was my attitude.

I got to the event and was pleasantly surprised. Did the rain bother the teenagers? Not on your life! There they were, dancing, having a great time with the music and the pouring rain, and up to their knees in mud. The wet weather didn't dampen their joy. And Monday was a fine and beautiful day.

Whatever day you're having, whether raining or not, alway keep your attitude right. Remember, there are some things a bad attitude can't change, but a good attitude will see you through. You can be a slave to your attitude or you can let your attitude free you.

A Missionary to Camden

A few years ago I was a guest speaker at a meeting in the United Kingdom. It was a convention of 30 to 40,000 people. Throughout the week a young girl was selling badges to raise support for herself. She wanted to be a missionary in Camden, New Jersey. She was selling the badges for 10p each (20 cents Australian). One of the badges was in the shape of a big heart which said, 'I love Camden.'

Now, if you know anything about Camden, you'll know it's not one of the loveliest places on earth. It's full of depression, violence and drugs. Yet this young lady seemed so full of joy, vision and zeal; she was selling these badges to support herself as a missionary. Her attitude was amazing; there was no victim mentality, none of the 'poor me having to go and struggle in this desperate situation'. She was full of enthusiasm and commitment. That's the attitude we need, even when we face almost impossible odds.

My guess is that the violence, hate and other problems of Camden still haven't affected her spirit. As a matter of fact, I *know* they haven't. Why? Because I know she chose to approach them with the right attitude.

The Upward Look

When our attitude changes, our problems take on a different light and we become free to feel more positively about them. Soichiro Honda said, 'I will become the Napoleon of mechanics.' He did. Napoleon said, 'I make circumstances.' As leaders, we must control our attitudes. Others count on us.

When leaders compromise their attitudes – when they allow, say, a spirit of mediocrity to prevail, whether in the office or at home – their whole organisation or family compromises. One cannot lead from an attitude of compromise. A healthy attitude towards life, people and difficult situations becomes an index of the greatness of our character.

Oscar Wilde once said, *'We're all in the gutter but some of us are looking at the stars.'* Leaders never compromise on their attitudes. The pessimist may be proved right in the long run, but the optimist has a better time on the journey! Richard De Vos, who has built a global business empire, has said this: 'Exhilaration of life can be found only in an upward look. This is an exciting world packed with opportunity. Great moments wait around every corner.'

Ten Powerful Attitudes

It might be argued that attitude is the sum total of the way we see events, people, the past and the future. Dale Carnegie says there are ten powerful qualities leaders must possess. Each one involves having a good attitude.

1. *Great leaders give praise and honest appreciation.*

2. *They call attention to people's mistakes indirectly.*
3. *They talk about their own mistakes before criticising another person.*
4. *They ask questions instead of giving direct orders.*
5. *They look the other person face to face.*
6. *They praise the slightest improvement and praise every improvement.*
7. *They give the other person a fine reputation to live up to.*
8. *They use encouragement.*
9. *They make a fault easy to correct.*
10. *They make the other person happy about doing anything they suggest.*

Every one of these qualities is outworked through a good, positive, purposeful approach. A leader cannot praise, correct, help people face-to-face, be an encourager or make people content and happy unless he or she has the right attitude.

Effective leaders understand that attitudes are caught, not taught. And they *are* contagious. A leader with a bad attitude, or a lack of courage, or an attitude of indifference, will be duplicated in his or her people.

'We're all in the gutter but some of us are looking at the stars.'
Oscar Wilde

The great golfer Arnold Palmer was once given some advice by his father, 'Remember, son, whatever game you play, 90% of success is from the shoulders up.' W. Clement Stone said, 'There is very little difference in people, but that little difference makes a big difference. The little difference is attitude. The big difference is whether it is positive or negative.'

Obstacles and Opportunities

What we are on the inside will affect what we do on the outside. The world mirrors our attitude within. If, as a leader, your world is dark, miserable, grey, lacking in vision purpose and direction, an attitude check is in order.

J. Sidlow Baxter wrote a wonderful book, *Awake My Heart*. It addresses the concept of attitude. He writes, 'What is the difference between an obstacle and adversity? Our attitude towards it. Every opportunity has a difficulty and every difficulty has an opportunity. If the best things are not immediately possible, then immediately make the best of things that are possible.'

> **'What is the difference between an obstacle and adversity?, your attitude'**
>
> **J. Sidlow Baxter**

One day a young man, Mal Hancock, experienced a tragic fall which left him paralysed from the waist down. A promising athletic career was left in tatters. The road to recuperation was all up hill. Heart-breaking times ensued as he attempted to make the necessary physical, emotional and mental adjustments in his life.

While in hospital, Mal developed a keen sense of humour about the things he saw and heard. He began to record them in the form of cartoons. It wasn't long before the staff would stop by to see what Mal had drawn. His cartoons became the centre of great attention. Mal eventually sold one to a magazine. It launched him into a career as a cartoonist. Now Hancock's cartoons appear in the *Saturday Evening Post, TV Guide* and the cover of his own book, *Hospital Humour.*

Mal learned he could not control the events of his life but he could control his reaction to them. He discovered the opportunities in the obstacles. Attitude is an incredible force which determines the outcome of life's crippling circumstances.

Dealing with Hurt

When I address people, whether young or old, I often ask for a show of hands from those who have been hurt. Then I ask those who haven't to fly around the room.

Hurt is part of every day life. How leaders view and react to hurt can make all the difference in the world. It is not wrong to hurt, but it is wrong to react negatively to hurt. I see many people who respond negatively to hurt. Leaders who seek to be credible cannot afford this luxury. I've seen leaders become bitter towards virtually everyone and everything. They view life through the prism of pain, hurt and bitterness, and eventually everything becomes distorted.

Hurtful remarks, hurtful actions and hurtful relationships can leave a bitter taste in the mouth and heart. But leaders can never be bitter and twisted. They can't afford bitterness because it sours everything around.

When it seems that others are more successful than you, do you react with bitterness? Or do you accept them for their success? It is always better to respond positively to the success of others. Who knows, it may rub off!

On the other hand, when you hear a bad report or rumour about yourself, how do you react? Do you want to lash out and attack? Or are you a person of action who goes ahead and keeps doing what you should?

How leaders view and react to hurt can make all the difference in the world

Reactionary leadership is a distinct problem. We must be able to control our emotions. Don't allow other's small-mindedness, petty thinking or negative comments to affect your attitude.

Keep Sweet

An irate adult once came to one of our young people's meetings. The music was loud, the lights were flashing and over 8,000 young people were screaming at the top of their lungs, having a wonderful time. There were no drugs or alcohol, just pure adrenalin – the encouragement and excitement of being with their peers.

Then this man stormed up to me. He was seething. He said he didn't agree with our frenzied music; to him it was all emotional hype. Then he lost it totally: 'Son,' he stormed, 'I don't like this Youth Alive thing!' I put a smile on my face and looked at him. I knew he was more than a little angry. I said, 'Sir, this is called Youth Alive, *not barely alive.*' And with that I walked away.

He was fuming, and one of my associates asked if I felt anger towards him. I said, 'No, never let anyone dictate to you how you react. Keep sweet at all times.'

How to Maintain a Positive Attitude

You're the cream of the crop, so don't let negativity, narrowness and small-mindedness turn you sour. Keep a good attitude and develop a *winning* approach to your problems.

Change Your Self-Talk

One of the ways to maintain a positive approach is to speak it. When you speak, it reflects the state of your mind. How many times have you talked yourself into attitudes, fears or sickness? Talk yourself out of these things, too.

The first rule of positive thinking is: *To change your attitude you must change your self-talk.* Rather than saying, 'I'm too old,' try 'My best years are ahead of me.' Our minds and bodies react towards our thoughts.

You Are What You Think

The second rule is: *You are what you think, and what you think, you are.* You will either master your thoughts or your thoughts will master you.

Everyone chooses what they think. Make sure your mind has a sense of direction and purpose. Don't wallow in self-pity for your failures or your dismal past; change your thinking. Here are some examples of negative thoughts to avoid:

- I'm hopeless.
- I'm a failure.
- I can't accomplish this.
- I'm inferior to other people.
- I'll never be able to do that.

Recently, I purchased a wave-runner. I was so excited about it – until I realised I had to back it into the water on its trailer. Feelings of terror surged within me.

I watched other men steer their trailers straight into the water. Needless to say, my experience was quite different. Every time I backed the car, the trailer would turn the opposite way. Then I straightened the trailer and reversed again. Finally one of my friends said to me, 'Pat, the problem is in your head.' Someone else had to back it in for me.

You will either master your thoughts or your thoughts will master you

Needless to say, today I can back my own trailer into the river. The problem *was* in my head. I needed to think straight in order to steer straight. It may seem like a simple thing, but it was my mind-set I had to change, not my steering.

Failure – The Back Door to Success

The real key to attitudes is not avoiding failure (because everyone will fail some time) but coping with failure. Our followers, constituents and mentorees understand this; they know we will fail. What they want to see is credibility in our attitudes.

Our attitude will determine whether we get up again and become a winner. If we do, we earn instant credibility. Our followers will also fail, but they will know we give failure its proper due. They will know we accept failure as a necessary evil on the pathway to growth. They will believe firmly we can be trusted not to reject them for failing.

The real key to attitudes is not avoiding failure but coping with failure

We must never crush our followers or make them drown in guilt for failing. If you constantly remind people of their failures it only rubs salt into an open wound. They need positive reinforcement and encouragement; they need to be taught, not beaten; and they need to be led and fed, not driven and starved of attention, encouragement and support. The leader's attitude determines the output of followers. The attitude which flows from words and posture will either build people up or tear them down.

Credible leaders always deal with others in a mutually constructive way. They approach everything with a win/win attitude. They learn to ask: How will these people following me feel? How can I express my feelings about this clearly without crushing them? Do I express my concerns in a concise manner, or do I approach problems in an irrational, harsh and destructive way?

Am I willing to coach others and see them through their failures and over their obstacles?

Asking yourself these questions will guide your actions and increase your credibility as a leader. It's amazing how your actions and disposition toward others will change with a small shift in attitude. A tiny shift in attitude can produce a huge shift in output. Leaders must either grow in attitude or shrink in significance.

ETHICS

To have true credibility with followers, leaders must be ethical. There can never be double- standards – one rule for them and one for me! People have to trust you to be there for them in the morning. Albert Schweitzer once said, 'Ethics is the maintaining of life at the highest point of development.' Individual ethics give depth and breadth to human relationships and are essential to growing big people.

Harry Gray, chairman of United Technologies, once said, *'It is without question that how we perform as individuals determines how we perform as a nation.'* This is true also in organisational structure. Personal philosophies of right and wrong will affect your organisation. It is the personal responsibility of leaders to instil, maintain and develop ethics in the organisation. Ethics will set an example for others to follow.

Every society has rules of behaviour to ensure survival. Some values once held dear in the past have been abandoned, to our own loss. Maughan once wrote, 'The great truths are too important to renew.' Ethics are always waiting to be found again by leaders. Being true to your word is never unfashionable; having pure motives is never out of vogue.

Ethical Questions

Consider the following ethical questions:

• You've had a busy day and you're sitting down to dinner with your wife and children. The phone rings. You tell your kids to say, 'Daddy's not home.' Later you try to teach your children that 'honesty always pays.' How do you explain telling the truth in the light of what you've just done?

• You are in a taxi and you ask the driver to head for your destination. You look down and see a wallet on the seat. Inside is a name, address and $5,000 cash. What do you do? Do you see it as heavenly provision and keep it? Do you ignore it and hope for the best? Do you do the right thing and report it to the closest police station?

• Here is a true life story from the *San Francisco Chronicle*. The back door of an armoured truck flies open. It dumps bundles of cash all over a busy street. The truck-driver speeds off unaware of what has happened. Dozens of people stop their cars and run from the sidewalk to chase the money being blown about by the wind. Some put it in their pockets and run; others gather the money and guard it until the police come.

What would you do? Would you have to think about it

for very long? Would it bother you that others have taken money and you have been left there to guard it? Would you feel at ease with the fact you have done what you think is right and watched over it until the police came?

Some ethical decisions – like those above – are fairly easy and relate to our natural responses to values impressed upon us from childhood. Other situations are very complex and difficult. How we deal with such issues shows the quality of our leadership and the level to which others can trust us.

'It is without question that how we perform as individuals determines how we perform as a nation'
Harry Gray

Having credibility requires being ethical. Tobacco companies advertise and deceive our young by depicting the use of tobacco as sensual, sophisticated and successful; they appear to do this without ever giving a thought to cancer or heart and lung disease. Consequently, tobacco companies have very little credibility.

If you can't deliver on time don't make a promise. Don't send cheques if you know they'll bounce. Don't lie or manipulate to get a deal. Don't play people off against each other in a negative or humorous way.

Just imagine what kind of world we would live in if everyone lived by high ethical standards – loving your neighbour as yourself; treating others as you would have them treat you; honouring the Ten Commandments (which these days appear to be treated as the Ten Suggestions).

Integrity is everything in leadership. One cannot expect others to follow or believe in a leader who is not as good as his or her word. Relational leaders must have high ethical standards; this is how we build trust with our followers, constituents and associates.

LIVING IT OUT

These then are the foundation stones of credibility. How does the relational leader build on them?

Here is a list of twenty behavioural patterns which, when practised by leaders, are guaranteed to engender loyalty, trust and credibility in followers. In fact, these are the twenty behaviours which leaders whom I have known and trusted have regularly practised.

1. *They have inspired me.*
2. *They have challenged me.*
3. *They have mentored me.*
4. *They have trusted me.*
5. *They have empowered me.*
6. *They have advised me.*
7. *They have taught me.*
8. *They have counselled me.*
9. *They have listened to me.*
10. *They have stuck to their convictions.*
11. *They have celebrated with me.*
12. *They have opened doors for me.*

13. *They have protected me from myself and from others.*
14. *They have corrected and rebuked me.*
15. *They have made time for me.*
16. *They have shared their visions, victories and credits with me.*
17. *They have given to me.*
18. *They have encouraged me.*
19. *They have not treated me as a threat.*
20. *They have cared for me.*

Our desire must be to demonstrate these very same characteristics in building trust and credibility with everyone around us.

Leaders who wish to have credibility will focus in on the key areas I've outlined. Here's a final checklist:

- Credibility is built on trust – people must trust you to follow where you lead.
- Trust requires accessibility – people need to see you.
- Credibility can never be maintained if core values go out the window, or if followers do not feel needed, wanted, valued and cared-for.
- Consistency is essential, both in maintaining a positive mental attitude (even in the midst of great difficulty) and in ethical life.

The effective relational leader knows how important it is to maintain credibility. It is the glue which binds followers and leaders together.

CHAPTER SIX

LEADERSHIP AND GROWTH

Growth in anything is not always an easy thing to achieve. Trees grow naturally and so do humans, but try convincing the CEO of a multi-national company that business is like that. Large growth comes in small steps, small, achievable steps. (Alcoholics Anonymous, for example, teaches people to stay sober one hour at time, one day at time. They know it's the small wins that count.).

Leaders who seek growth set goals that are reach-able. They know never to set goals so high they can't be attained. Sometimes, leaders set standards beyond the abilities of their followers – and even themselves – to reach. If no one can reach your standards, maybe the bar is too high. Perhaps you need to break the goal up into smaller, more easily achieved steps and more readily attained goals.

A friend told me the story of how he got the members of his youth group to become book readers. As you know, a lot of young people are reluctant readers, so he started a competition. This competition had very strict rules, and everyone had to abide by them to the letter. If anyone broke the rules they were immediately disqualified. What followed was amazing.

Here's what he did.

To enter this competition everybody had to buy from him a particular book. When the books were purchased they were wrapped up tight in their shopping bags. The

Large growth comes in small steps

young people didn't know the name of the book they were about to read and had no idea of its contents. Under no circumstances were they to open the bags and look.

After a couple of days they were allowed to unwrap them. That doesn't sound very exciting, but my friend had created a hunger and an expectancy. However, still they weren't allowed to read the book.

The next step was to open the book and close it. They were not to read anything or browse through or even skim the contents – just open and close it. They had to do this three times a day for three to four days. Can you imagine the frustration for some of those kids?

Next my friend had them open the books and read

one sentence – no more, no less – three times a day. After a few trying days of this he permitted them to open the book and read one paragraph – no more, no less – three times a day. If anyone read more than a paragraph, he or she was immediately disqualified.

By this stage the kids were in a frenzy. He had created such a hunger in them they began to get frustrated with the leader. They wanted to go on and find out the contents of that book! He let them move to a page at a time. Next came a chapter at a time. Finally the entire book was consumed.

Here's the growth he achieved:
1. He created a hunger to read that wasn't there before.
2. He aroused their curiosity to find out the next step.
3. He encouraged them to memorise through repetition.
4. He created a knowledge of what was going on in the books and a sense of anticipation.

My friend successfully created a hunger to learn more through his unorthodox system. He created growth in people who would have resisted it if he had tried to communicate this value by any other means. Eventually the entire youth group became a group of leaders. In developing readers, he had developed leaders.

And it all happened little by little, in small incremental steps.

How Growth Occurs

Leaders bring out the best in people and produce growth in them. Their role is to see the potential within followers and grow it. Leaders can produce growth in others with a simple word, a note of encouragement, a sentence of insight and inspiration. This is how leaders grow big people.

To produce growth we first need to know how growth comes about. Here are some of the ways:

1. *Life experiences teach growth if we are willing to listen.*
2. *Good solid relationships stretch you and sharpen your abilities.*
3. *Leaders are readers – books produce growth.* There is a wealth of knowledge to be found in consuming good books. Read all kinds of books, both books you agree with and books you disagree with. Don't be afraid of contradiction. Challenge it and let it sharpen your wits.
4. *Listen to tapes produced by wise speakers who have grown and learned through experience.* Sometimes you get from a tape what you can't get from a book – the emotion and soul of the speaker.
5. *Difficulties and hard times teach you how to act and react.* Difficulties teach you both how to be strong and how to handle your emotions.
6. *Winning teaches great lessons.* You are never too old or successful to learn the things which lead to victory.
7. *Trial and error can be a great teacher.* Only fools do

not learn from their mistakes. The poet Archibald MacLeish once said, 'There is only thing more painful than learning from experience, and that is not learning from experience.'

8. *Education and training produce growth.* Whether in the classroom setting or through mentoring on the job, education is the information and training which produces growth.

9. *Observation is a great teacher.* Learn from watching others, and growth is sure to follow.

10. *Be a listener with both ears.* Don't be an ineffective listener, only hearing what you want to hear and filtering out what you don't. What you need to hear can often be very painful, but it also produces growth if responded to correctly. Learn to listen.

GROWING IN RESPONSIBILITY

There are many areas in which leaders must grow, but the chief of these must always be responsibility. Leaders must grow in their responsibility and care for others, which means that leaders cannot stand still. There is a growth curve in leadership and its called 'learning.'

When leaders refuse to grow they no longer deserve to be leaders. It is immoral to

'There is only thing more painful than learning from experience, and that is not learning from experience.'
Archibald MacLeish

condemn others to the level of your own mediocrity. No one will follow an irresponsible leader for long. Inspiration stems from responsible leaders.

Like it or not, a leader is responsible for everyone's growth. The buck stops here. Every leader is a steward of other people's lives, and leaders cannot delegate all their tasks and responsibilities away completely. Of course, there are always going to be instances of things that leaders cannot control; you are not responsible for the sun coming up in the morning or for the ebb and flow of the tides. But you must take seriously the things you can be responsible for.

So, relational leaders must accept responsibility both for their own lives, and for the lives of those they lead.

Responsibility for Yourself
Living in regret

Leaders must never live in regret, looking back to lost opportunities. Every opportunity must be grasped as long as it's today. I read somewhere, 'Nothing is more painful than regret'.

If you accept responsibility you never have to live with regret

Some years ago, the truth of this was brought home to me. I was very close to a brilliant speaker, a guy who could move an audience from laughter to tears in ways I've seen few people able to do. He had brilliant content, gifted communication and a great future.

Tremendous opportunities opened up all over the world. He seemed to have it all. His motto in life was 'No regrets.'

I'll never forget the day I called his house and asked to speak with him. The little boy on the other end of the phone said, 'I'm sorry, Pat, Daddy doesn't live here any more.' When I challenged my friend about the innocent relationship which had caused his marital breakdown, his broken promises and hurting kids, all he could do was blame his spouse and his children for not understanding how gifted he was, how busy he'd been, and how much he had done for them. He failed to accept responsibility for his actions and, worst of all, must now live with the regrets.

Being a leader means accepting responsibility for actions – and if you accept responsibility, you never have to live with regret.

Responsibility frees us. Accepting responsibility is never a hindrance to the true leader. This is all the more startling because responsibility doesn't end until leaders quit leading. Learn to grow in responsibility and never seek to avoid it. Be responsible for your own actions.

Responding to hurt

Leaders are responsible in how they respond to hurt. If someone hurts you, analyse whether that hurt was intentional or not. Not every hurt is an attack, nor are they all vindictive attempts to destroy you.

At the end of the day, you are responsible for your

reactions to the deeds (and misdeeds) of others. For example, only you can control how you speak. A lot of friction in our daily lives is caused by the way we say things, not necessarily the way people hear things. We are responsible for our words.

Forgiveness
One of the great ways to demonstrate growth in responsibility is by *showing forgiveness*. Everyone fails – even you – so everyone deserves a little grace. Big people are built up by grace.

> *'If you're suffering from a bad man's injustice, forgive him lest there be two bad men.'*
>
> **St Augustine**

Like it or not, you are responsible to forgive people. St Augustine once said, 'If you're suffering from a bad man's injustice, forgive him lest there be two bad men.'

Responsibility for Others
It is the leader's responsibility to secure the future of others. Don't leave it to chance or luck. You've got to be mindful of your mission and follow through on your plans and promises. You can't control how others react, but you can keep your own attitudes and actions in check. The ability to improve, adapt, change, develop, maintain a positive attitude, keep a sense of humour and be courageous are all responsibilities of leadership. Not using gifts and talents is irresponsible.

Responsibility entails action. This fact distinguishes leaders from followers – true leaders know what to do, and do it; followers may know what to do, but may not do it. When you remind a teenager to do homework or be on time, the response you get is amazing: 'I know, yep . . . I know.' But getting them to do what they know is a different story.

The difference between knowing and doing is called a growth-need; it's the gap between the doing and the talking.

The ability to enhance, improve and develop is another quality that puts leaders ahead of followers. Leaders need to look around and ask: What do my followers need to do in order to grow? Any old formula won't necessarily work; after all, people are all different, with individual personalities, skills, dreams and visions. Leaders must not only create an individual environment for growth but the requisite opportunities, too. This has much to do with planning and people management – how to get the best out of every individual.

Growing Big People

Leaders who seek to grow big people must do the following:

1. *Ask: what is the strategy for growth?*
2. *Be willing to change, to keep growing by moving onward and upward*
3. *Be an example of growth*
4. *Assess what growth will cost*
5. *Challenge people to grow*

6. *Allow them to grow*
7. *Release them to grow*
8. *Plan for their growth*
9. *Monitor and acknowledge their growth*
10. *Don't be threatened by their growth*

GROWING IN COMMUNICATION

Having created a plan for corporate and individual growth, however, leaders are often faced with a great challenge, one which requires growth in themselves: to communicate their plans and aspirations.

One of the most chronic leadership weaknesses is expressing ideas. Failing to grow in communication skills can make an otherwise good leader ineffective.

There is no point communicating from on high what is not understood at the grassroots

Quite often human beings find it hard to express themselves, yet communication is a vital key for fulfilling our purposes and strategies.

Effective relational leaders understand the process of communication. The word 'communication' comes from a Latin root meaning 'to commune' – to hold in common. Communication is and will always be *people talking with people so that they understand what is being said.* There is no point talking to your followers in a foreign language, and there is no point communicating from on high what is not understood at the grassroots.

Leaders who communicate well produce growth in followers, in business and in their personal and professional lives.

Aspects of Communication

Communication plays a big part in growth. The following are important aspects of communication:

1. Leaders must understand the people or person with whom they are communicating. One doesn't need to be an expert on personalities, but one needs to understand how certain personality types think and can be motivated. People are unique. I highly recommend Florence Littauer's book Personality Plus. When dealing with groups, watch body language and facial expressions. Try to set people at ease, whether you are speaking to a group or an individual.

2. Keep in mind some practical tips on communication:
   - *Know your topic.* People can spot vagueness immediately.
   - *Look at people.* Develop eye contact.
   - *Bring your audience to a point of ease and relax them.* Tell a story, tell a joke (preferably not a corny one).
   - *Make sure you like your audience.* Fall in love with your listeners and they will fall in love with you. People resist aggression, especially public aggression.
   - *Illustrate and apply what you're teaching.* Don't just give out concepts, show how they work and how to apply them.

- *Be confident.* Confidence stems from knowing what you're saying is true and worth following.
- *Involve your audience.* Get them to laugh or make some kind of noise. People love interaction. Use gestures, smiles, facial expressions.
- *Don't overload them with information.* Use the 'KISS method' – Keep It Simple, Stupid.
- *Be authentic.* Dr Wayne Dyer says this is the first rule of speaking. It's important to speak from the heart and not just the head.

Communication and Credibility

As we saw in the last chapter, credibility is vital to success in leadership. The most important quality you have is your credibility. Without credibility you communicate in vain, because how you live speaks louder than anything you say. People follow your actions more than your words. Your grand vision for growth can be stifled by a lack of credibility. Credibility communicates loudly before you ever open your mouth.

When you are communicating your plan for growth, be very aware of your assumptions about the people you're trying to communicate with. Personally, I've fallen into the trap of buying into too many assumptions, to my own disappointment. Assumptions are not proven facts and often have no basis in reality. We may be second-guessing, prejudging and committing a host of other communication 'sins' against our followers.

I will never forget speaking to a colleague who was continually second-guessing me. There is nothing on earth more frustrating than someone telling you what you're thinking – especially when they're way off beam. *Put yourself in another's shoes.* Don't try to *put them in your shoes.* Put yourself in their place and think how you would respond.

Tact

Growth can be painful, so when sharing your master vision, remember that one of the qualities of good communicators is tact. **Mr** Tact communicates his thoughts with sensitivity to the atmosphere and the moment. Tact is all about thoughtfulness towards others and is a combination of interest, sincerity and caring. It certainly isn't blundering in where angels fear to tread.

Put yourself in another's shoes. Don't try to put them in your shoes

There's an interesting story about a very tactful shoe salesman. A lady with rather large feet came to him seeking help. Rather than abruptly stating her feet were too big for the shoes she wished to purchase, he put it this way: 'I'm sorry we don't have your size. It seems these shoes are just too small for your feet.' Tact and diplomacy say 'the shoes are too small,' not 'your feet are too big.'

Leaders need not become politicians, fearful of making or communicating tough decisions. But they do need to use care and sensitivity when communicating, the kind they desire to have shown to themselves. People are not mind-readers. Your staff, teams, clientele or family do not know your every thought.

You must communicate clearly. Someone has said, 'A problem well stated is a problem half solved.' Clear expression of a problem, a plan or the central issues of a situation will go a long way to achieving growth. Ill-advised or poorly expressed sentiments certainly never assist anything but failure.

Reactionary Communication

Communication must never be reactionary. Leaders often see and hear things which make their blood boil, but *too bad* – that comes with the territory. The rule is:

Act, don't react

Reaction shows emotion out of control; action shows someone in control. It takes a big person to keep acting on their dreams and goals rather than reacting to criticism or others' insecurities.

> *'A drop of honey attracts more flies than a gallon of gall'.*
> **Abraham Lincoln**

There was once a politician who had won many elections. He was a man of integrity and honour, held in high esteem in his town. A young upstart ran against him in the local elections. In trying to win the people to his cause, the young man started to attack the prominent senior politician, falsely accusing him of wrong actions and underhanded dealings. The senior politician's P.R. person said, 'You've got to make a stand against these things, you've got to tell the truth. Tell them this man is lying.' The older man responded, 'Have you ever seen a dog bark at the moon? The dog barks loud and makes a lot of noise, but the moon keeps on shining.'

No matter what happens to you or is said about you, choose never to react. Just keep on shining like the moon. Abraham Lincoln once said, 'A drop of honey attracts more flies than a gallon of gall'.

Listening and Speaking

Dorothy Neville made an interesting comment about communication: 'The real art of conversation is not only to say the right thing in the right place, but to leave unsaid the wrong things at the tempting moment.' That is tact and diplomacy, knowing when to speak and when to keep quiet.

> 'The real art of conversation is not only to say the right thing in the right place, but to leave unsaid the wrong things at the tempting moment.'
>
> **Dorothy Neville**

Just as important is knowing when and how to *listen*. Never underestimate the power of listening as well as the power of words. Communication is both listening and talking; it involves both words and silence. To be a good speaker and communicator one must first grow into a good listener.

Leaders must be very careful to hear what is going on all around them. Only then can they accurately assess situations and implement changes. Abraham Lincoln said, 'When I'm getting ready to reason with a man, I spend one-third of my time thinking about myself and what I'm going to say and two-thirds thinking about the other person and what they are going to say.' He spent two-thirds of his time thinking about the other person; he was more interested in listening than speaking.

Peter Drucker adds a further thought: 'The most important thing in communication is to hear what isn't being said.' That's an even deeper level of listening, one requiring perceptive hearts as well as perceptive ears. Communication doesn't start with leaders being understood, but with leaders trying to understand others.

Communicating with Your Heart

I love something John Maxwell says: 'To handle yourself, use your head. To handle others, use your heart.' Maxwell is correct. In communication, emotion is a vital key. Use your heart, not just your head, and you will influence others for good.

To communicate with your heart, remember the following:

The six most important words: 'I admit I made a mistake.'

The five most important words: 'You did a good job.'

The four most important words: 'What is your opinion?'

The three most important words: 'If you please.'

The two most important words: 'Thank you.'
The most important word: 'We'
The least important word: 'I'

The author of this is, sadly, unknown – but he or she was very wise. This is the greatest communication advice I've ever read.

Communication with the heart means using our words carefully. Our words should build others up, not pull them down. Our words should inspire them to action. Our words should input for the future, not deflate and drag them back into the past. Our words should be timely, not hurried. Remember, in communication a sharp tongue and brilliant mind are never found in the same skull.

> *'To handle yourself, use your head. To handle others, use your heart.'*
> **John Maxwell**

Finally, choose your words carefully to ensure people understand. One of the funniest communication stories I've heard concerns a lady called Joan, who was speaking to her neighbour over the fence. Joan said, 'The events of our household this past week have left me in a state of consternation.' Her caring neighbour quickly adviocd her, 'Why don't you try prune juice?'

Communication can go wrong. Leaders are in the growth business, and growth requires good, clear communication; so, ultimately, successful relational leaders will be good communicators.

GROWING IN WISDOM

Leaders must grow in wisdom if they are to help others be wise. It is possible to grow in wisdom. Wisdom comes with experience and knowledge; both go hand in hand.

Unfortunately, we can easily try to apply wisdom to others even when it's lacking in our own lives. It is a wise leader who heeds his own advice and acts on it.

One of the world's greatest repositories of wisdom is the biblical book of Proverbs. Here is just a short synopsis of what it says wisdom does for us:
- It brings understanding.
- It gives instruction.
- It gives prosperity.
- It helps us avoid evil.
- It gives an increase in learning.
- It helps us set boundaries.
- It creates discipline.
- It gives discernment.
- It brings happiness.
- It gives confidence.

Knowledge and Wisdom

There is a major difference between knowledge and wisdom. Many knowledgeable people do very unw e things. Community youth workers, for example, seem very knowledgeable about the problems of drug abuse, but often, sadly, they cannot apply such knowledge to their own addictions.

Wisdom is the *application* of knowledge and truth. We live at a time when knowledge is increasing at an incredible rate, yet if one looks at the modern lifestyle, many unwise decisions are devastating communities, businesses, churches, homes and marriages. People are not using wisdom when they speak or deal with others.

Leaders must grow in wisdom if they are to help others to be wise

Wisdom is thinking ahead, knowing what to do next. Wisdom is the ability to discern – it is insight and perception into varied and difficult situations. It is the ability to recognise problems before they become total catastrophes.

Gaining Wisdom

How do we gain wisdom? We gain wisdom through life's experiences and by cultivating relationships with trustworthy people.

Mentors give us wisdom, which is why I am such a strong advocate of mentoring as a role and responsibility of leadership. Looking for people who care about you and understand your desires, dreams, strengths and weaknesses is the place to begin the search for wisdom. Such people will be straight with you. You can't grow in wisdom unless people help you – and, in turn, you will never grow big people yourself without wisdom.

Having those around you who ask the hard questions

or put you in the right frame of mind is not always easy, but it is imperative for the leader of the future. Leaders need to grow, so mentoring is essential. Wisdom isn't found overnight.

Learning from Wise People

A simple starting point for those who wish to become wise is to read autobiographies of successful people. No one ever gained success without wisdom, so read about people of vision, people of character, people who understood the cost of success.

Wisdom is the application of truth and knowledge

Such people will be creative, goal-orientated people, serving others, hungry to grow, brimming with confidence, constantly encouraging, always active. Significant people – the type good biographies are written about – will be strong people, respectful people, generous people and godly people. They will be worth reading about and they will help you grow in wisdom.

Having a Voice

Effective leaders use wise words to speak into peoples lives messages which drown out the echoes of complaint, slothfulness, distraction and discontentment. As we look around, the influence of TV, the other media, misguided pop stars and the Internet is all-pervasive, voicing unwise messages which destroy or influence

young people for ill. Such messages destroy free thinking, even as they claim the power of liberation; they neither motivate nor convict. Rather, lacking in wisdom,
they promote unwise behaviour – a lack of morals, a
continuous search for direction and a frustrated, empty
way of living.

Wise leaders influence the mind, the emotions and
the dreams of people, rather than supporting the negative, empty voices of our fast-paced, politically correct,
value-lacking popular culture. Growth in wisdom means
knowing when and where to take a stand to influence
others for good.

GROWING IN INFLUENCE

There is a connection between wisdom and influence.
As you become wiser, you will have greater influence on
others. Therefore, seeking wise people to help you is a
must if you want to be influential yourself.

To influence is to deposit
something in others which
brings change or affects decisions. Many politicians have
advisers, men and women who
influence the decisions of leadership. They also influence
people all around them in reciprocal relationships.

*Good leaders have
influential people
all around them*

If there are no such reciprocal relationships there is
no leadership. Leaders are a part of what's going on;
they don't live apart from what's going on. Leadership

is not about dictating or throwing weight around. It's about gaining credibility through relationship, then using that relationship to communicate a plan for growth in the best possible way. The image of the superior boss and inferior follower is a thing of the past.

Being influential means being wise in how you use words, tapping into people's dreams, goals, ambitions, desires and knowing how best to achieve them. To do this well wisdom is key, for without wisdom it is impossible to set the individual plans necessary to grow big people.

Leadership is Influence

President Harry Truman, in speaking on the influence of leaders, said this: 'A leader is a person who has the ability to get others to do what they don't want to do and like it.' Fred Smith, my favourite author, says, 'Leadership is influence.'

It's imperative to surround yourself with people of influence so that you can become a person of influence. It is easy to look around and see the influence leaders have. Take Bill Gates, for example; one only needs mention his name and automatically the ideas of computers and communication spring to mind. Henry Ford profoundly influenced the automobile industry; Michael Jordan has influenced basketball and sport in general, not to mention advertising. Mother Teresa, Nelson Mandela, Ray Crock, Colonel Sanders – all have influenced the world.

Influence is important and good influence requires

wisdom. Bad influence can do great harm; as the biblical phrase puts it, 'If a blind man guides a blind man both will fall into a ditch.'

Affecting the Now

Wise, influential leaders affect the now. They also affect the future and help us to understand that present impossibilities are merely ill-defined possibilities which we can beat if we go the extra mile, make the extra effort, think creatively and avoid living in boxes.

Wise influence produces growth. It assists in launching others out into the deep water with their own self-defined plans for success –

Leadership is assisting others to reach their own peak

plans which, in the long run, will assist them to fulfil their dreams. And that is precisely what leadership is: assisting others to reach their own peak.

Wise Reference Points

When a leader grows in wisdom, he or she becomes a reference point for followers who wish to grow into big people. A leader of influence is a model. Others will copy and imitate this reference point. How often do you hear someone quote Michael Johnson or Carl Lewis? Such people are finding reference points in these successful men and are beginning the patterning process.

People who become successful in any field soon themselves evolve into reference points for others.

Often when an Olympic record is broken, it is broken again soon afterwards. This has happened even where the initial record has stood for twenty years or more. Why? Because a new bench mark has suddenly been created, a new reference point for others who wish to follow in the footsteps of the great.

It's amazing how quickly people believe new records can be set, new goals achieved, new heights scaled once someone has been successful and become an influential reference point.

Forerunners and Pioneers

Wise and influential leaders are often forerunners and pioneers, the first to scale an impossibly high mountain. By being so, they cause others to stretch out and reach for new heights. Then growth results.

A pioneer goes before others and leads the way into fields of new opportunity, unlimited possibility and the conquering of unconquerable obstacles. When an influential leader picks up the shovel and breaks new ground, others follow in his or her pioneering ways. Because they are out on the edge, wise leaders can often be misunderstood. Their motives can be questioned. People of influence will always be attacked by those who are happy to run the institutions and maintain the status quo. Institutions keep things manageable and comfortable – confined in their own little boxes.

Leaders are consumed by a passion

Influential leaders cause people to break out of boxes to scale further heights.

William Booth

General William Booth, the great founder of the
Salvation Army, was frowned upon by the religious leaders of his day. He was even called a charlatan by some.
Yet at the funeral of Catherine Booth, his equally
famous wife, the influence of the Salvation Army was so
enormous that more people attended her funeral than
attended Queen Victoria's.

Like William Booth, any leader who seeks to influence others for the good will not be content to live in
the realm of maintenance. They will be consumed with
a passion for progress and growth, to go where no one
has gone before. Growth then inevitably occurs in those
who follow them, for in such pioneering circumstances
people will be released in their potential. There won't be
time for fussing and fighting; people will be too busy
achieving.

Growth at McDonald's

If I were to say to you the employees of McDonald's
grow constantly, you would probably answer, 'Oh, yeah,
they grow hugely – right round their waistlines.' But do
you appreciate what this influential company actually
achieves with its staff?

John Love wrote a book, *Behind the Arches*, in which
he comments: '4.5% of the American work force has
worked for McDonald's. One in every 15 American
workers go to his/her first job for McDonald's. While
most of those work elsewhere, it was at McDonald's
where they first learned about work routine, job disci-

pline, and organisational team work.' Can you believe that? Four-and-a-half per cent of Americans grow vocationally today because someone had the vision of mass-produced hamburgers. It may not be your vision or mine, but you get the picture. Someone led and people started growing.

IMPEDIMENTS TO GROWTH

Always remember there are several impediments to growth, and leaders make these mistakes as readily as followers. The chief of these is feeling threatened.

Never be threatened by the success of your peers or followers; it stifles growth.

The marks of the threatened leader are:
1. *Pulling people out and 'putting them in their place.'*
2. *Rejoicing over others' failure.*
3. *Suppressing and stifling creativity and free-speech.*
4. *Giving verbal rather than heart-felt encouragement.*
5. *Being fearful of others' success.*
6. *Pulling others down.*
7. *Making him or herself big at other people's expense.*
8. *Bullying.*
9. *Being defensive and protective of his or her own patch.*
10. *Remaining distant and aloof.*
11. *Taking all the credit.*
12. *Being unnecessarily competitive.*
13. *Embarrassing others and criticising publicly.*

14. *Attacking ability, dignity and performance inexplicably.*

The non-threatened or influential leader
They produce growth in followers in the following ways:
1. *Bringing people into their rightful place.*
2. *Getting in their place and bringing them up to scratch.*
3. *Grieving at others' failure and showing them how to succeed.*
4. *Releasing gifting and creativity and encouraging diversity.*
5. *Giving positive encouragement and backing it with practical input.*
6. *Riding on success, encouraging it and associating with it.*
7. *Pushing others to the top.*
8. *Making others big at his or her own expense.*
9. *Encouraging through difficult times.*
10. *Being open and vulnerable.*
11. *Being a friend.*
12. *Sharing credit around.*
13. *Being competitive in a positive way.*
14. *Praising publicly and correcting privately.*
15. *Protecting performance and leaving dignity intact.*
16. *Recognising and encouraging ability.*

What Type of Leader are You?
Leadership is not about rulers and subordinates, masters and slaves. It's not about management skills or hav-

ing the right structure. Leadership is about building a sense of community, ownership, family and accountability.

Leaders are credible servants, supporters, coaches and partners. Rank does have privileges, but wise leaders never rely on power to get things done. Leaders never work through bribe and threat; no one grows into greatness that way. Leaders seek to grow in wisdom themselves so they can identify needs and develop plans and programs for the growth of every individual following them. Having done so, they seek to communicate these plans effectively and with love.

Rank does have privileges, but wise leaders never rely on power to get things done

Make no mistake. Leaders have no almighty, divine power bestowed by position. Leaders can achieve very little by the exercise of strict power. Influence – wise, growth-oriented influence – is something earned through trust, warmth and credibility. Leaders first grow themselves, then seek to grow others.

Leaders cannot expect the best from followers with respect to quality time or service if they treat them as inferiors. Such actions never bring out the best or cause growth. Leaders who create a sense of community, loyalty and honesty, who communicate clearly with followers, bring out the hidden growth in others. This is how big people are created.

What type of leader are you?

CHAPTER SEVEN

THE LEADER AS FRIEND

Friendship is a key factor for any leader. The proverb says, 'Two are better than one – there is more reward for their labour.' You will never be an effective relational leader or a good mentor without first learning how to build simple human relationships.

I began this book with a discussion of leaders and their relationships with followers. I went on to look at mentoring, which implies an existing relationship. I've talked at length about being a 'relational' leader. By now it should be obvious that I firmly believe in leaders building relationships with their followers. There is no function of leadership not dependent on this.

Reading that may surprise you, especially since many leaders have been trained in the old school which said,

'Never fraternise with followers.' To do so was seen as somewhat demeaning for leaders. Such a model cannot survive the 1990s.

In this chapter, I want to focus your attention on friendship, and especially on how it bonds leaders to followers and allows for the growth I've spoken about to occur. It's fine to talk about growth and growing, but in what precise context can it happen? I believe the context is *friendship* – mutual and equal.

John D. Rockefeller once said, 'A friendship founded on business is better than a business founded on friendship.' Your job is not to fill up your social calendar wining and dining your work colleagues but to build meaningful, growth-producing relationships.

Friendship is the essential model for successful leadership in the 1990s

I am convinced that friendship is the essential model for successful leadership in the 1990s. If you intend to grow big people, this is where you start.

The Importance of Friends

The friends you surround yourself with will be the friends who influence you in your thinking and decisions. One of the great examples of a person influenced negatively by unwise associations was US President Richard Nixon. He listened to the counsel of untrustworthy people and received the due reward.

Beware your associations. Emily Clemstine once

said, 'Be careful the environment you choose, it will shape you; be careful the things you choose, you will become like them.' I would add: Be careful the associations you choose. One rotten apple can spoil a whole barrel.

However, good relationships never damage you. George Eliot once said, 'Friendship is the inexpressible comfort of feeling safe with a person, without needing to weigh thoughts or measure words.' And Henry Ford was known for saying, 'My best friend is the one that brings out the best in me.'

Everyone needs friends. They are the essence of what it means to be human and to have communication skills. We are creatures made to commune with others. Friends are a security, an island of safety and a rare and special treasure. Leaders must never take friends and friendship for granted, but rather should work hard on these relationships.

A Man with No Friends

Without friendships, our lives are filled with alienation and disorientation. Howard Hughes, one of the richest men in the world, died friendless.

Thousands of people had their destiny determined by this man, yet he lived an empty, crazy life. His beard came down to his waist; his hair reached the middle of his back. His fingernails were two inches long and had not been trimmed for so long they resembled cork screws. He was married for thirteen years to Jean Peters, one of the most beautiful women in the world, but never were they seen together in public. They had separate rooms in the Beverley Hills Hotel and were divorced in 1970. He often said, 'Every man has his price or a guy like me could never exist.' Yet, no amount of money bought him friends.

Why was he so alone? Simple. He never learned to build friendships or enjoy other people. He was too busy manipulating them to befriend them.

What Friendship Isn't

Using people is definitely not what friendship is about. Nor is it just a matter of being on first name terms with someone or sharing the same office. Many people assume acquaintances are friends. They're not. Friendship is quite different.

Leaders must never take friends and friendship for granted, but rather should work hard on these relationships

Leaders need more than mere acquaintances. They need friends willing to go the extra mile.

Friendship is not just about being near to people, either. My greatest hero is Jesus Christ. He had many people close to him. One of them, Judas, kissed him and another of them, John, put his head on his chest. But Judas kissed him because he was going to kill him, and John put his head on his chest because he was willing to die for him. Both were close, both were affectionate, but only one was a true friend.

In leadership there is a need to discern between your basic Judas and your basic John. I want to help you find the Johns of the world, so I propose to introduce you to one of the world's great friendships, documented for us in the Bible: the friendship between Jonathan and David.

PRINCIPLES OF FRIENDSHIP BUILDING

When one thinks of Jonathan, one thinks of one of the most interesting characters of ancient Israel. The son of the nation's first king, King Saul, Jonathan displayed many of the characteristics of the true friend. These characteristics are what good leaders look for in their friends. They are also the qualities good leaders cultivate in themselves.

Souls Knit Together

The first thing we learn from young Jonathan is that his 'soul was knit' to his friend David. Their souls were knit together.

Picture this: Young David – ruddy, good-looking and covered in lambs' wool clothing – has just come back from killing a giant called Goliath. He's covered in sweat and blood. He walks into the king's tent still carrying Goliath's head dripping blood on the floor.

Talk about decorum and manners! This isn't the way you approach a king! How many of us would have a chance of getting into Buckingham Palace, the White

House or the Prime Minister's office looking like that? However, I notice something about Jonathan, the king's son. He's totally indifferent to this. David is dressed like a beggar and a pauper; Jonathan is dressed in royal garments. David is poor; Jonathan is rich. David has been brought up in a field; Jonathan in a palace. But, when Jonathan looks at David, Scripture says their souls were knit together.

A Common Cause

As different as these two young men were, it is here we find the first principle of friendship- building. *They had a common cause.*

If one looks at the life of Jonathan, one finds his father, King Saul, to be a bitter, angry man. David's father Jesse, on the other hand, didn't even acknowledge he was around. When the prophet Samuel first came to look among Jesse's sons for the man who would replace Saul as king, David was out looking after the sheep. His father and brothers had forgotten him.

Making common cause with your followers benefits all concerned

It's important to understand that Jonathan and David had a common interest: they were both suffering rejection from their fathers. Although this is a painful experience, it highlights their mutual attraction. You never hear Jonathan or David whining or being negative about their fathers. They never mention it. They never discuss their pain. But it linked them together deeply. In a similar way, if you want to build lasting friendships with people, you need to share with them some common goals, common aims, common values, common principles and common beliefs – or as I prefer to call it, *a mutual attraction.*

Jonathan's friendship ensured Saul's hatred of David never materialised into actual physical harm. If you build quality relationships with those around you – particularly with your followers – such relationships will protect you from harm.

Making common cause with your followers benefits all concerned. Your followers will warn you of danger, assist you in hard times, motivate you when you're down and contribute to your success – all because you are a friend to them.

Sharing Success

The second thing I notice about Jonathan is that he shared his success with David. When David walked into the royal palace in Jerusalem, Jonathan made him a special promise of friendship and gave him his own robe.

If you want to build lasting relationships with people, make sure you're not afraid to share your success with them. Jonathan took off his fine royal robe and gave it to David, a sweaty, blood- covered shepherd boy. In life, if you're successful and you want to build good friendships, you must be willing to share your success with others, and willing to welcome them into your 'palace.' It's important to be generous with friends.

Don't be Threatened

Jonathan, in putting his robe on David, shows that he is neither threatened by David's great military success nor jealous of it. He's not concerned to look better than David, even though his self-effacement actually contributes to David's success.

A sign of a leader's security is that their peers and friends can be as successful as they are

Destroying relationships is easy. Petty jealousies and threatened and insecure leadership destroy the mutual benefits of friendship. A sign of a leader's security is that their peers and friends can be as successful as they are – and even more successful – and they enjoy this.

Giving up your Armour

At the same time as Jonathan gave David his robe, he also gave David his armour. What does this speak of? Protection.

A faithful friend protects you by watching for impending danger. Some people say they are friends, but when the fiery darts of adversity come along, rather than warning and protecting, they put others in the line of fire.

We need to protect our friends from impending dangers such as gossip and rumour, ensuring we put armour around them – the armour of accountability, protection and encouragement.

Delighting in Friends

Jonathan delighted in his friend David. Jonathan's father, Saul, personally tried to kill David and even told his servants and soldiers to pursue him. Yet Jonathan – knowing his friend would be king one day – told David about his father's plans, and rather than assisting the lethal scheme, protected him.

A faithful friend, whether a leader or follower, is one who is more interested in protecting you than in having a position over you. Never put position before friendship.

I can remember working on a particular committee. Many of the members were dissatisfied and wanted me to take over as leader. However, the chairman of the committee was one of my closest friends. I chose instead to speak on behalf of the committee to let him know people's concern in a loving way. I made my intentions very clear: I would never go for the chairmanship of that board. Even though I knew that the committee and the team needed fresh leadership and vision, I did not want to be the one to put the knife in, turn it and take over.

A faithful friend, whether a leader or follower, is one who is more interested in protecting you than in having a position over you

This was difficult and very painful for me, yet to this day we are still the closest of friends. Though it was a tough situation, my aim was to protect him and his dignity, not take away his position. In the end, the appropriate measure was to ask him to stand down. This proved to be the correct one, and it never hindered our relationship.

Giving up Your Sword

Jonathan also gave David his sword. David now knew if ever a sword came against him, it would not come from the hand of Jonathan. I often say, beware the man who won't give you his sword.

If a friend has 'given you his sword,' then when someone speaks against you, you will at least know where it *doesn't* come from. Leaders must know where criticism, stabs and attacks *don't* come from as much as where they *do*. I've seen men and women in positions of leadership accuse followers of various acts of disloyalty and faithlessness, even when it wasn't the case. Leaders who have friends know when they get cut, it wasn't by the hand of their followers.

It's important to have the kind of friends who won't stab others in the back; and if you want to be treated that way, then you also have to not stab others in the back. You need people around you who won't attack you but will help you because you're a trusted friend.

So, do what it takes to build the kind of leaders around you who are loyal and will protect you. In short, become a true friend to your followers.

Shielding Others

Jonathan protected David by giving him his shield. This

pictures beautifully the value of being open and vulnerable. I also warn leaders to beware of people who won't drop their shields.

Have you ever got close to someone, thinking you've found a window into their lives but then suddenly hitting a wall? It's possible, even in leadership positions, to shut up shop and keep others at arm's length. But this never creates true intimacy. Often leaders hide because they are afraid or embarrassed or threatened. They build walls instead of windows.

> *Beware the man who won't give you his sword*

Leaders must drop their shields but not their guard. In other words, there is nothing wrong with trying to protect yourself – just don't be so closed that you fail to build honest, whole relationships with others.

Loyalty

One of the things which made the friendship between Jonathan and David so special was their bond of loyalty. Their loyalty was based on a promise – the promise of reconciliation.

Thanks to David's popularity after the defeat of Goliath, King Saul became intensely jealous of him. Over the next few years he violently persecuted David. But Jonathan tried continually to reconcile his father to his best friend.

A loyal and true friend will always put you in good standing with others. They will help build bridges with others. Leaders can hurt people both unintentionally and intentionally, but a true friend will always make you aware of the situation and not capitalise on it for personal gain. True friends try to repair the bridges which have been torn down.

Keeping Promises

One of the promises David made was that when he became king, he would never harm Jonathan's family. Years later, long after Saul and Jonathan had been killed in battle and David had become king, David remembered this promise.

A leader who is a true friend will always keep his promises

He asked if there was anyone left from the 'house (family) of Saul' to whom he could show kindness 'for Jonathan's sake.' Someone remembered one of Jonathan's sons, five years old when Jonathan was tragically killed, and a cripple. David found him, a beggar on the street. He brought him into his own house and appointed workers to work the fields to make money for him. Then David told him that, as long as he lived, he would eat at the king's table. David restored to him all the land that had rightfully belonged to his father and grandfather and made him an equal in the house of the king.

There are several important lessons that wise leaders will learn from David's treatment of Jonathan's house:

1. *A leader who is a true friend will always keep his promises.*

2. *Leaders look after their friends and care for their interests, even if they have been discarded and forgotten.*
3. *Leaders are not afraid to be associated with the tragedy of others, nor are they lacking in the compassion to help when tragic circumstances hit their friends and families.*

Loyalty doesn't start with followers; it starts with leaders. It is handed down and passed on. It flows from leaders to followers. Encouraging loyalty in our corporations and businesses is a simple as us showing loyalty.

Friendship should never be based on negatives but on positives, and loyalty is the great positive on which we can build a friendship.

FRIENDSHIP AND LEADERSHIP

Leaders will always be good friends – if they want to be successful, that is. Cathy Mohnke has said, 'Friendship is like vitamins, we supplement each other's minimum daily requirements.' Your friendships will impact much of what happens to your leadership.

Unfortunately, today's concept of friendship is often more like the TV variety, lacking in direction, values and true loyalty. But good leaders realise they have the ultimate power to choose what type of relationship they will have with followers.

One of the Proverbs tells us that if we want friends in life we must be seen to be friendly. But that isn't always easy. Friendships in business and leadership do not just happen; they have to be built.

Friendship, like leadership generally, requires honesty, integrity and commitment to promises, even when it hurts. It also requires leaders to be personally growing, moving forward and committed to their relationships with their followers. And again, just like leadership generally, integrity and accountability are key.

In other words, the responsibility for developing friendships does not reside with others but with us. As individuals and leaders, we must seek to be friends and foster friendship with others. *We* must learn to cultivate openness with friends. *We* must learn how to harmonise with others.

Learn to be a Friend

The Beatles once sang, 'I can get by with a little help from my friends.' It's not only important for leaders to find the right circle of friends; it's also important for them to become the right kind of friend themselves.

Often people say, 'If I could just hang around more successful people I would be successful.' That's quite true. But successful people tend to run with successful people. This is so with friends, too. If you want good friends, you must first be a good friend.

Similarly, sometimes people question their partners in life, saying, 'Perhaps if I had another woman or man, things would be different.' 'Things' probably wouldn't be different at all, because you yourself would still be the same. The basis of our problems is us, not others.

So, if you want good friends, learn to be a good friend. Why not start by asking your colleagues, your business associates, your employees or mentorees, what they are interested in? Show some interest in what turns them on. Make a fuss of them when it's their birthday or when they show initiative. If you find out one of your followers is an avid fisherman, send him a new fly-rod for his birthday – that's how friendship begins.

Good leaders think less of themselves and more of others. President George Bush once said, 'Use power to help people. We were not given power to advance our own purposes nor to make a great show in the world, nor a name. There is but one just use of power and that is to serve people.'

John Maxwell has said, 'Leaders must be close enough to relate to others, but far enough ahead to motivate them.' To be a great leader means to know how to build friendships with others while still being the strong, visionary initiator.

> **'Leaders must be close enough to relate to others, but far enough ahead to motivate them.'**
> **John Maxwell**

Remember, friendship is the key ingredient which will allow you to build the big people you need to make your organisation successful.

CONCLUSION

PERSONAL GROWTH AND EFFECTIVE LEADERSHIP

This book has been all about leaders growing up into their full potential, so it would be wrong of me not to conclude with some final words about growth – my favourite subject. Every person needs to grow in life and leadership. Refusal to grow does not even permit us to stay at our present level of success and productivity; it causes us to go backwards. There is a degenerative effect. We are either growing or dying, but we never stand still in our surroundings. The reasons are twofold:

- Other things are moving ahead while we stagnate
- Anything that doesn't grow soon dies – growth is natural

The How and Why of Growth

The *how* of growth and the *why* of growth are both important. Nature itself teaches us that if a plant in its early growth stages, grows on an angle – if it's either leaning to the right or the left, or if it's not staked properly – it will develop a growth pattern in that area. Rather than growing straight, it may lean to the right or the left, so a stake must be planted into the ground to assist the plant to grow effectively – just the way it's meant to grow. This must happen early in its growth, because *how* it grows is as important as *why* it grows. The same applies to leaders. *How* leaders grow is as important as *why* they grow.

Growth is Relative

It's always as important to keep in mind that all growth is relative – it all depends on comparison with other things. Even though everyone needs to grow and go on growing, many people feel they have reached their peak. However, one person's ceiling is another person's floor.

Take the example of income. Some feel they have reached their peak and couldn't possibly go any further. If you think like this, consider a Chief Executive's income level. As large as his or her income may be, most of the **good** ones have not reached their peak. If you think they have reached their peak, compare Rupert Murdoch with Bill Gates. There is always another level. The same is true of personal, motivational, educational or intellectual growth. If you have reached your 'ceiling' you will either bump your head or break through and move up to a brand new level. Growth is vital because we need to grow *into* our future. Only then can we bring maximum growth for our organisations; only then can others follow with respect. Growth is a *growing into*, a *growing up to* and a *growing up for* – the genuine 'because' of growth.

Growth is a Journey

Any leader who feels he or she has arrived has actually never travelled in the first place. When we refuse to address issues of personal growth in any area, we stifle our growth. Leaders who don't **give** sufficient time, thought and input for growth to happen, will stifle themselves and their organisations – they will put the brakes on corporate and private success.

Many leaders fail to understand that no position is permanent; there are levels of growing into and progress in, and there are also downward spirals in leadership. There are knocks and bumps and bruises to growth, but there is not one thing in life more valuable than human growth. Just think of the areas in life growth touches: influence, profitability, values, home-life and success. These all depend upon nurturing and growth.

Leadership Skills are Transitory

Everything is transitory; everything moves and evolves. Our leadership skills are transitory, needing constant honing and improvement. Our level of success can transition into greater growth, greater productivity and an even greater sense of achievement. Leaders who want to be successful need to understand their strengths and limitations. Leaders will discard weaknesses by working on them, and hone a sharper edge on their strengths to attain new levels of success.

Leaders hungry for growth will review their performance, their involvement, their successes and their failures. We can learn from the past and our commitment to growth can help shape the future. Max DePree says, 'We cannot become what we need to be by remaining what we are.' Another wise man once said, 'It's never too late to become what you might have been.'

Robert Schuler once said, 'Either you are expandable or expendable.' Leaders, is your life habitual or experimental? Are you just into a habit without breaking a comfort zone,

Our leadership skills are transitory, needing constant honing and improvement

without trying something new or something fresh? Just remember, the old saying – 'that's the way we've always done it' – has been the ruin of many people's personal growth. We need to keep pushing down the walls of the comfort zones which restrict ideas and zeal, and which close the door to new opportunity.

What You are Right Now

What you grow into and become as a leader is far more important than where you are right now. Each of us, if we are careful to monitor growth and feed ourselves, will become better than we are right now. I once heard someone say, 'Life only gets better when you do.'

Former American President, Harry Truman, once said 'Life is iffy'. We enjoy life more *if* we expose ourselves to the unfamiliar. We become more valuable *if* we are growing and stretching. Work is more fulfilling *if* we decide to be our best. The *ifs* are endless.

Growth is Exciting

Zig Ziglar puts it this way, 'Go as far as you can see and when you get there, you will always be able to see further.' At some business functions, I have watched people receiving recognition and had the privilege of observing their growth into levels of leadership, responsibility and greater success. Their whole world seems to change around them. Their countenance changes; their personal dress and attention to detail changes; their confidence changes. They've gone a little further down the road, and they see a little further into the horizon, and they want to grow into it.

Becoming What We are Meant to Be

Remember, we are becoming what we are meant to be. This requires a hunger to learn. No person ever grows unless they are willing to listen and learn. It doesn't matter what level you've achieved in life, everybody can learn more. That's why it's imperative to read, to listen, to talk, to have a mentor to look up to and follow. One must be humble enough to receive direction, strong enough to receive input and, if necessary, to receive constructive criticism (I hate that term).

There are elements of my present role as leader that would not only have destroyed me and others, had I been responsible for them even a few short years ago. I wasn't ready. I needed to learn how to handle staff, how to control budgets, how to handle money, how to deal with people and their various personalities. If I had been given these things 10 to 12 years ago, I would have made a total hash of them.

Although my potential for leadership was always there, I had to grow up into the position, and the position had to grow up inside me. I had to learn. All of us must take the view that we are leaders in process and people in progress. J.C. Penney once said, 'No one need live a minute longer as he is because the Creator endowed us with the ability to change ourselves.'

> *No person ever grows unless they are willing to listen and learn*

What Hinders Growth?

Some leaders fail to grow, and there are numerous reasons for this. Here are a few things to watch out for if you're serious about growth:

* Some leaders think they don't need to grow. The

basic issue here is pride. They feel they have arrived and no one can teach them any more.

- Some don't see their future clearly and, therefore, don't see the need to grow into their future.
- Some adopt the 'been there done that' mentality.
- Some are unwilling to.
- Some fear that they may not like what they will become. Their present position gives them a sense of security and comfort.
- Some fear the disciplines and changes to be made and refuse to engage with the process.
- Some get no input through books, tapes and listening to other successful people.
- Some are never shown the areas they need to grow in.
- Some think it's a long hard process and they're right – it is. It is a process and it takes time.

The Goose which Lays the Golden Egg

When thinking about leadership, always keep in mind the fable of Aesop, *The Goose and the Golden Egg*. It's the story of a poor farmer who visits the nest of his goose and finds a glittering yellow egg. He thinks it's a trick and is about to throw it away, but thinking better of it, takes the egg home. To his amazement he discovers that the egg is solid gold.

The farmer becomes increasingly rich by going to the nest daily and collecting a golden egg from his special goose. As he grows richer, he becomes greedy and impatient. Hoping to get all the gold and riches, he kills the goose and cuts her open only to find ... *nothing*. The lesson behind the fable is: to think that one can grow in one single swoop is deceptive, destructive and only results in losing rather than winning. It's the daily activities, the daily disciplines, the daily shoulder to the wheel and the daily checks which cause us to grow.

Leading and Reading

I know I have said it before, but leaders are readers. The effective leader keeps reading, storing up a wealth of wisdom and example for the difficult times. To grow leaders must read. The person who can read but does not has no advantage over the person who can't read at all. Reading is a necessity, and not only so because we read truths and go through them, but because we let the things we read go through us.

The largest room in the world for any of us is the room for improvement. The way to improve is to grow. In this book I have listed many areas where leaders need to grow. We have looked at motivation, effectiveness, mentoring strategies, as well as growth in integrity, in people skills, in family life and in relationships. If you really want to become the leader you can be, then let growth happen. Grow and move on from achievement to significance, and on to great success both as a person and as an effective, relational leader.

I wish you well,
Pat Mesiti
January 11th 1998